BOOK OF DAYS

AN EASTER BOOK OF DAYS

Meeting the Characters of the
Cross and Resurrection

I. BIBLE
II. HISTORY
III. TRADITION
IV. FAITH

Gregory K. Cameron

PARACLETE PRESS
BREWSTER, MASSACHUSETTS

2022 First Printing This Edition
An Easter Book of Days:
Meeting the Characters of the Cross and Resurrection

Copyright © 2022 Gregory Cameron

ISBN 978-1-64060-857-3

Originally published in the UK under the title
An Easter Book of Days
by the Canterbury Press, an imprint of Hymns Ancient & Modern Ltd of 13a Hellesdon Park Road, Norwich, Norfolk NR6 5DR

The Paraclete Press name and logo (dove on cross) are trademarks of Paraclete Press

Library of Congress Control Number: 2022944744

10 9 8 7 6 5 4 3 2 1

Published by Paraclete Press
Brewster, Massachusetts
www.paracletepress.com

Printed in Korea

CONTENTS

For my diocese,
a faithful network of colleagues, friends
and disciples of the Crucified God.

INTRODUCTION

In my earlier ADVENT BOOK OF DAYS, I produced twenty-five meditations to take the reader through December in preparation for Christmas. This is less easy for Easter, not least because the feast day itself slips around our calendar in pursuit of Passover. There is Lent, but forty-six meditations could be unwieldy. Although there are many characters involved in the story of Jesus' Passion, death and Resurrection, an attempt to produce a reflection for every day might use up the entire cast. In this book, I offer twenty-five meditations, not linked to specific days, to Passiontide or Holy Week, but rather reflections that may be read at leisure in the period around Eastertide.

There is another complication in the nature of the characters we encounter. A Christian poet once wrote that the characters of Christmas carried 'a hint of rich perfume', whereas Easter brings with it 'whips, blood, nails, a spear and allegations of body snatching'.[1] The characters we meet are complex. They are sometimes cast in the role of villains or conscripts. There is ambivalence, and some of the darkest themes ever to cast shadows across the Christian faith. Nevertheless, here are twenty-five characters, creatures or places for whom there is a rich tradition, and I have adopted the same method as in

---

1 Steve Turner, 'Christmas is Really for the Children', 2003.

my Advent book, by approaching them through the lens of the Bible, history, tradition and faith.[2]

The inspiration of the medieval books of hours is repeated here. Each chapter begins with an illustration adapted from the great works of Christian art across the centuries, from the sixth century to the contemporary world, so that each reflection opens with a *visio divina* to prompt and focus the reader's thoughts.

I hope that this book will assist you to encounter the richly woven fabric of the story of the Passion, and the experience of Jesus and the first disciples. It will draw you into a very human drama, but also one in which divine grace and power are at work. Those of us familiar with Anglican or Catholic liturgies will know the form of 'the Mystery of Faith' in the Eucharist, which says, 'Dying, you destroyed our death. Rising, you restored our life. Lord Jesus, come in glory.' The story of the cross and Resurrection draws us into a personal relationship with the characters of the Passion, and invites us to be transformed just as the earliest disciples and followers were transformed by the experience of Jesus' death and resurrection.

+*Gregory Llanelwy*
Ascension 2022

---

2 I'm indebted to the *Church Times* for suggesting 'Tradition' as a better word than the original 'Legend', when they serialised the Advent Book in their newspaper in December 2021.

ONE

THE CROSS OF THE SAVIOUR

I

For many, the worst calamity is death. Yet Christianity had to face up to the fact that one death was at the heart of anything it wanted to say. The disciples of Jesus believed that he was the Messiah, the chosen one of God, the Saviour of the World, and yet the culmination of his life was death. The death of Jesus is so important for the Gospel writers that it absorbs most of their energy. The story of the last seven days of Jesus' life (sometimes called Holy Week) takes up almost a third of the Gospels of Matthew and Mark, a fifth of Luke's Gospel, and almost half of John's Gospel. It is as if the most important thing they had to explain was Jesus' death on a cross, a subject that crops up in virtually every book of the New Testament.

The cross therefore, in myriad different forms, is historically the paramount symbol of the Christian faith. The earliest symbol of Christianity was the fish, arising from the happy coincidence that the Greek word for 'fish' spelt out an acronym of the earliest creed of the Christians, 'Jesus Christ Son of God Saviour'. This was a more secure symbol in days when Christianity was persecuted, and the brutal punishment of crucifixion was still current. As the centuries passed and divided Christians from the immediacy of the crucifixion, however, representations of the cross began to appear, although at first in highly abstract form.

The depiction of the cross I have used here is one of my favourites, set in a mosaic of the twelfth century in the apse of the Basilica of San Clemente in Rome. I like it because it fuses the image of the cross with another powerful image that Jesus offered of the Kingdom of God in Luke's Gospel (13.19). Jesus speaks of the growth of the Kingdom of God as like a mustard seed, so tiny that it can scarcely be seen but growing into a tree so mighty that all the birds of the air come to lodge in its branches. In this mosaic, the cross becomes a tree in which all can take shelter and find salvation.

As centuries passed, Christians felt bolder depicting the suffering of Christ, and pictures of the crucifixion became more graphic, often reflecting the times and circumstances in which they were composed. In the time of the Black Death and later, pictures of extreme bleakness and suffering were produced culminating famously in the sixteenth-century *Crucifixion* by Grünewald at Isenheim. Not all depictions of the crucifixion are as harrowing and the cross has also been fashioned in gold and jewels and fine art. In words attributed to Kublai Khan, the

Chinese emperor, 'you Christians have taken an instrument of torture and turned it into a thing of beauty'.

III

When the emperor Constantine adopted Christianity in the fourth century, his mother, Helena, made a pilgrimage to the Holy Land with all the resources of empire at her disposal. One of her early projects was to find the True Cross. Having interrogated the locals in Jerusalem, Helena came to the conclusion that the emperor Hadrian, some two hundred years before, had deliberately obscured the site of the crucifixion by building a pagan temple over it. Digging there, Helena's workforce are said to have found three crosses – hardly surprising since Jesus had been crucified between two thieves. How could she choose between them? Legend says that she brought a woman close to death into contact with each of the three crosses. On touching the tree of life, the woman was restored to life and health, and so it was that Helena identified one of the most prized relics of Jerusalem. This event was even given its own feast day, 'The Invention (Discovery) of the Holy Cross', still celebrated in places on 3rd May.

Helena's cross was set up for the veneration of the faithful on the site Helena believed was Calvary and it remained there until captured by the Persian emperor Khosrau in 612 AD. The emperor Heraclius of Rome was able to win it back seventeen years later, and he set it up again to much rejoicing so that this event also got its own feast day, the Feast of the Exaltation (or Triumph) of the Cross on 14th September.

After that, the history of the cross becomes murkier. It was said to have been hidden from the depredations of the Muslim ruler Al-Hakim in the eleventh century, and only fragments were rediscovered later by the Crusader priest Arnulf. Today, the True Cross has no clear location, but fragments of wood claiming to be of the cross are preserved throughout the world. There is great cynicism about whether any of them can be traced back to the real thing, and some people claim that there are enough relics to create a dozen crosses. I was told as a student, however, that a Cambridge Professor had undertaken the task of cataloguing every relic of the True Cross known to exist. All put together made up not more than a third of a full-sized cross. That's the lovely thing about Christian tradition – we can never quite be sure that its core is false.

IV

These stories matter because they illustrate the centrality of the cross to Christian faith. In theology and worship, the death of Jesus is not merely a death but 'a full, perfect, and sufficient sacrifice, oblation, and satisfaction, for the sins of the whole world', to quote a Christian liturgy. As Christians meditated upon scripture, one passage of the Old Testament in particular stood out for them – Isaiah Chapter 53.2–6:

> He had no form or majesty that we should look at him, and no beauty that we should desire him. He was despised and rejected by men, a man of sorrows and acquainted with grief … Surely he has borne our griefs and carried our sorrows; … he was pierced for our transgressions; he was crushed for our iniquities; upon him was the chastisement that brought us peace, and with his wounds we are healed. All we like sheep have gone astray; we have turned – every one – to his own way; and the LORD has laid on him the iniquity of us all.

For believers, this unlocks the mystery of why Jesus died, and so terribly. The cross becomes the place where all the darkness of the world, its sins, failings, and horrors, are taken on by God and borne by Jesus. As we're told that the apostle Paul later wrote: Jesus cancelled 'the record of debt that stood against us with its legal demands. This he set aside, nailing it to the cross' (Colossians 2.14). This is not, as sometimes portrayed, a vindicative God having to punish someone for the sins of the world. Christians believe that 'in Christ God himself was reconciling the world to himself, not counting their trespasses against them' (2 Corinthians 5.19). In other words, God accepts all the pain and cost of what is wrong in the world by carrying it himself. He dies on the cross that we might be forgiven.

Easter is a time of paradox. We celebrate new life, but only by facing up to a death. We acclaim the love of God but revealed in the most brutal and bloody of events. We are brought to the foot of a place of torture and shame, only to discover that it is a place of victory. In John's Gospel, Jesus' last words are: 'It is accomplished.' No wonder then that Christians make an instrument of torture into a thing of beauty. As we conclude this chapter, let us pause for a moment to reflect on the price of God's great love for us, such that he humbled himself, even to death on a cross.

Lord God, help us to face up to the mystery of your love revealed in the cross; a place of pain and yet the place where peace is made between God and humanity. In Jesus, you stretch out your arms in love to embrace me and to offer me love in the place of judgement, healing in place of failing, and hope in the face of regret. Amen.

TWO
THOMAS THE DISCIPLE

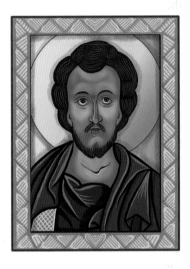

The Christian story of Easter is about the work of God in defeating sin and raising new life. It is a story of transformation for all disciples of Jesus, and perhaps none exemplifies this better than Thomas.

I

One of the compelling things that leads me to believe that the Gospels are trustworthy is the way in which the disciples are portrayed so honestly as vulnerable and wayward. Thomas is the disciple who appears to be the pessimist among the Twelve. It is Thomas, who, when it becomes clear that Jesus is heading to Jerusalem, says: 'Let us also go, that we may die with him' (John 11.16). It is Thomas, who when Jesus has proclaimed his identity as the Way, the Truth and the Life, asks: 'Lord, we do not know where you are going. How can we know the way?' (John 14.5). Like most of the disciples, Thomas struggles with the journey of faith, and most famously, when the Resurrection takes place, it is Thomas who declares that he can't believe it and demands evidence (John 20.25).

The resurrected Jesus seems to know such things, and when he next appears to his disciples, Thomas is picked out for special attention. The risen Jesus still bears the wounds of crucifixion which he offers to Thomas for his inspection (John 20.24ff). Thomas' response is immediate and transformed. He confesses his faith, hailing Jesus as 'My Lord and my God!'

II

Nearly all we know of the disciples historically is from the New Testament. Some of the earliest Church historians, writing a couple of hundred years later, offer us a few more details. Eusebius, writing in the fourth century, tells us that Thomas went off to preach the gospel in Parthia, what would today be the area around Afghanistan. Tradition, as we will see, tells us that he went much further. Egeria, one of the first Christian pilgrims, about the same time as Eusebius, tells us that she made a detour especially to visit the Tomb of Thomas, set up in a Church in Edessa, in what is now southeast Turkey. Today, there are claims that his relics are interred in Abruzzo in Italy. Very little can be reliably proved.

The fact that Thomas was such a human disciple, however, has made him a very popular saint. We can identify with him. The picture I have chosen for today is an adaptation of a modern Syriac icon of Thomas, and many Middle Eastern Christians identify with this disciple and his journey of faith.

srl

One intriguing discovery in the twentieth century was the unearthing of a 'Gospel according to Thomas' among the archaeological remains of Egypt. This had not made the grade to be included in the New Testament by the early Church, who ruled out any book that they felt did not have strong enough evidence of apostolic authorship. Much of its text includes parables and other sayings that appear in one or more of the four recognised Gospels, but it does not attempt to tell the story of Jesus' life and death, and is rather a haphazard collection of sayings. It reminds us that the early Church community cherished the memories of Jesus' teachings, and that, as John admits (John 21.25), not everything made it into the Gospels as we have received them. Luke in the Book of Acts, for example, has Paul quoting a saying of Jesus not recorded in any of the Gospels (Acts 20.35).

III

Tradition tells us that Thomas went all the way to India (and some say even further to China). There are strong links with Thomas in India, and a number of ancient church buildings which claim that they were founded by Thomas as he travelled to and settled in Kerala in India. These include a tomb at Mylapore, where it is said that Thomas was martyred by the local King, Gondophernes. At least three contemporary Indian Churches claim descent from St Thomas: the Malankara Syrian Orthodox Church in the Oriental Orthodox family, the Syro-Malabar Church, which is in communion with Rome, and the Mar Thoma Syrian Church, which has close ties with the Anglican Communion. This historical continuity is perhaps the strongest living witness of Thomas' claim to be the Apostle of India.

Thomas is the archetype of the disciple who passes through a journey of faith, plagued by doubt and prone to misunderstanding Christian teaching, but whose encounter with the living and resurrected Christ brings him to faith. Jesus is the person who changed Thomas' life, and his encounter with Christ after the Resurrection set him on a path of lifetime commitment.

Thomas teaches us that to be a disciple is not a counsel of perfection. We are not expected to pretend that we are without doubts, neither are we required to master every small part of Christian faith and practice in order to qualify as disciples of Jesus. The heart of our faith is an encounter with the living presence of Jesus through prayer and Word and Sacrament. Through these, God's grace and love can touch us and transform us, as they did in Thomas' life. As Jesus said to Thomas: 'Have you believed because you have seen me? Blessed are those who have not seen and yet have believed' (John 20.29).

Let us reflect for a moment on our own discipleship, which might be so like that of Thomas, wanting to believe and yet needing help with the stubbornness of our unbelief.

Lord Jesus, help us to be like Thomas, and to confess you as our Lord and God. Teach us to be honest in our faith, not afraid of doubt or when we fail to understand, but able to prioritise love as the fulfilling of your law. Amen.

THREE
LAZARUS

As Jesus approached the last week of his life, he arrives at the home of old friends on a very personal mission. Who is Lazarus, and what is his significance for the story of Easter?

I

There are several references in the Gospels to a group of friends of Jesus who are members of the same family. They appear to be a family of three, two sisters, Martha and Mary, and a brother, who is given the name of Lazarus in John's Gospel, but called Simon the Leper in the Gospels according to Matthew and Mark. Several events tie the members of this family together in the ministry of Jesus, but the most significant of them involves the death of Lazarus.

This story is told in chapter 11 of John's Gospel, and is the last of seven 'signs', or miracles that point to the identity of

Jesus. This Gospel is carefully constructed so that these signs punctuate the teaching ministry of Jesus, and each one reveals a little more about the identity and mission of Jesus.

Immediately before we go into the story of Jesus' last week, we are told the story of Lazarus. At first, Jesus is informed that Lazarus is gravely ill, but seems unconcerned. Eventually he arrives at their home in Bethany only to discover that Lazarus had died and has been buried for four days. Jesus, however, calls Lazarus out of his tomb, and Lazarus answers and comes forth. The picture that I have chosen for this chapter is adapted from a seventeenth-century Russian icon, and it shows Lazarus, still clad in his grave clothes, standing in the entrance of the tomb, unable to resist the summons of Jesus back into life.

As the story unfolds the sisters have a discussion with Jesus about the nature of death and the promise of eternal life contained in the Scriptures. In response to Martha's scepticism, Jesus reveals himself: 'I am the resurrection and the life. Whoever believes in me, though he die, yet shall he live, and everyone who lives and believes in me shall never die' (John 11.25, 26). In other words, the raising of Lazarus reveals Jesus in the clearest way as the one who opens the way to eternal life, the master of death itself.

II

The significance of this miracle is reasserted in John 12.10, 11, where the evangelist writes that this miracle convinced many of the reality of Jesus' claims, and caused the authorities to seek Lazarus' death. It is this miracle that seems also finally to make up the minds of the Jewish authorities that Jesus must be removed. Reports of Jesus' miracle are carried back to the chief priests and the Pharisees, who are brought together by their opposition to Jesus. 'From that day on', John records, 'they plotted his death' (John 11.53).

Such a story appears to be confirmed in Jewish writings. The Babylonian Talmud and an obscure Jewish text, 'The Book of the Life of Jesus', tell the story from the other side, although we have to approach them with great care. The Talmud is a collection of Jewish traditions, brought together in the beginning of the sixth century, while many scholars regard 'The Life of Jesus' as a work from the medieval period, although it may contain much earlier traditions. What interests me is that these documents do not deny the exceptional nature of the story of Jesus. They speak of Jesus as a great miracle worker but one who achieves his miracles as a sorcerer. When Jesus raises a person from the dead, the Jewish authorities combine to sentence him to death. For forty days his condemnation is proclaimed, until he is finally captured and hanged just before the Passover. Are there echoes here too of the apparent raising of Lazarus dividing people in their judgement of Jesus, and which provokes those opposed to him to seek his death?

III

Today, the town of Bethany is known as Al-Eizariya, 'the place of Lazarus'. Legend tells us, however, that Lazarus and his sisters had to escape persecution. Eastern tradition has the family travelling to Cyprus, where Lazarus became the first Bishop of Kition, while Western tradition has him and his sisters adrift upon a boat and washed up on the shores of southern France. Here, he is reputed to have become the first Bishop of Marseilles, although he faced persecution under the Roman emperor Domitian, and was beheaded in the prison at Saint-Lazare. Rather bizarrely, while his body is said to be buried in Autun Cathedral, which is dedicated to him, his head remained in Marseilles. Autun became a great centre of pilgrimage in the medieval period, and Lazarus a witness to the healing ministry of Christ.

IV

Lazarus is the saint whose own resurrection points to Jesus as the herald of eternal life. Jesus, about to travel to Jerusalem for his passion, reveals through the miracle of the raising of Lazarus that he will conquer the power of death, and invites all who follow him to share in the new life that he brings.

There is also significance in the details of the story. Jesus raises Lazarus only four days after his death. Martha, at least, had despaired that the situation could be rescued. Yet Jesus keeps faith with the sisters and acts. The story in John chapter 11 contains the shortest verse in the Bible: 'Jesus wept' (John 11.35), and this speaks to us of our Lord's compassion for his friends and for humanity. When Jesus has brought Lazarus back to life, he commands that he is released from the bindings of his shroud.

John deliberately calls the miracles of Jesus 'signs', because we learn something of Jesus' significance from every action in them. Here, we learn that Jesus cares deeply for each one of us as a disciple, and that we should never feel that the situation has gone beyond the ability of God to intervene, even if it is in ways that we do not expect. God seeks for us to be unbound by the things that can restrict us and confine us to a smaller life. By the power of resurrection, we are called into a life of the glorious freedom of the gospel.

Let us be quiet in the presence of Jesus, who brings new life to his disciples, and let us ask for a new beginning and the renewal of our journey of faith.

Lord Jesus, you are the resurrection and the life. Help us to find new life in you. Free us from the failings and sins that can confine us, and open out for us the fullness of eternal life. Teach us to seek your help even in the most extreme of circumstances, and give us the gift of faith. Amen.

FOUR
MARTHA & MARY

In John's Gospel, the raising of Lazarus triggers the events of the Passion. Jesus' friendship with the family of Lazarus, however, is the safe haven from which Jesus sets out on his final mission. John 12 records a dinner party for Jesus immediately before the events of Holy Week begin.

I

At this dinner John records a woman called Mary anointing Jesus with expensive perfume. This appears both to trigger Judas' betrayal of Jesus, as he is depicted as disgusted by the wastefulness, and Jesus' own recognition that his death is at hand: Mary, he says, has anointed him for his burial. Jesus' friends at Bethany therefore play a pivotal role in Jesus' ministry, even if we can't be certain whether this Mary is the same person as the member of Lazarus' family.

The Gospels set the two sisters of Lazarus in antithetical roles. Mary, if she is the pourer of the perfume in this story, is usually depicted as unquestionably faithful in the stories told about them, while Martha has a harder edge. At the raising of their brother Lazarus, Mary is the one who professes her faith in Jesus' miraculous power, while the practical Martha, although believing in the resurrection of the last day, the day of judgement, is very basic and uncompromising about the reality of her brother's death.

The most famous story about the sisters, however, is told in Luke's Gospel, at the end of chapter 10.

II & III

Jesus is staying with the family, and again a meal is held in his honour. Martha dedicates herself to the hospitality and is upset when Mary stops to listen to Jesus. Martha asks Jesus to tell her sister to help, but gets rebuked by Jesus. Mary has chosen the one needful thing, and Jesus won't tell her to stop listening to him. It is this scene to which I have alluded in the picture that accompanies this chapter. Adapted from a traditional Russian icon, it shows Mary enraptured listening to Jesus, while Martha, with her sleeves rolled up for work, and washing up in hand, looks more distracted.

The lesson seems obvious. Mary chooses the needful and better role of spending time with Jesus rather than fussing about the details of the meal, while Martha misses the point by rushing around to get the meal sorted out.

Some of the greatest early Christian theologians, however, have been more generous in their assessment. St Ephrem, a Syrian theologian of the fourth century, stated that Martha's love for Jesus was the more fervent, since she prepared ahead for the visit of the Saviour, and was ready to offer service to him, while St Augustine also commends Martha's readiness to assist the saints and disciples that accompanied Jesus. St Ambrose reminds us that saintly virtue does not have a single form whether it be busy devotion or pious attention, although both he and Augustine stress that while Martha is concentrating on the temporary, Mary is focussing on the eternal.

IV

I must admit that I have always had my sympathies with Martha. Her very name suggests that she was the elder sister, and in charge of the household – Martha is an Aramaic word that means 'the mistress' – and it was her duty to ensure that Jesus and the guests at dinner were well provided for. We know from John's Gospel that she was a person of faith, and probably committed to doing her best for Jesus. She serves in the best way she can, and yet Jesus also backs Mary's desire to learn.

Rather than seeing these two sisters in opposition, I think it is better to see them as exercising ministry in complementary ways. The word used of Martha's busyness is in Greek that same word that is used for the deacon in the Church, so there is just a hint that Martha is one of the leaders of the early Church. She is the living embodiment of Jesus' teaching that the greatest of his disciples would be the ones who made themselves of service to the Church and the world. 'The greatest among you shall be your servant' (Matthew 23.11). Equally, discipleship cannot all be 'mission'. We have to be dependent on Jesus, and that includes our readiness to learn, so that Jesus commends Mary's desire to listen to his teaching. This is still intriguing. In Jewish tradition, the men listened to teaching, while the women laboured at hospitality. Jesus is quietly asserting the status and position of women among his followers. They too are welcome to access his learning in an equal role.

This quiet little family in Bethany therefore teach us many lessons. Discipleship is both service and listening to the Lord, and women have equal status with men in Jesus' family of disciples, an egalitarianism that the Church has not always managed to respect. As we close this reflection, let us thank God for the path of discipleship, and that all people – male and female – are called equally to follow Jesus.

Lord God, thank you for the ministry and witness of both Martha and Mary. May we be like them, keen to be active in service, and yet dedicated to listening to teaching of Christ. May we be a community in which men and women are called equally to discipleship and service – in Jesus' name. Amen.

FIVE

JERUSALEM

All the events surrounding the Passion (a cover-all term that encompasses the arrest, trials, crucifixion and death of Christ) take place in Jerusalem. Why is this so significant, and what is the place of Jerusalem in the story of Jesus?

I

In the Bible, Jerusalem has unique significance as a city. It was captured by King David in approximately 1000 BC from the original inhabitants, the Jebusites. Jerusalem, located on Mount Zion, was understood as the place that God had chosen uniquely as his dwelling place on Earth. It is celebrated in the Psalms, and the story of its recognition as the capital city of God's people is told in the historical books of the Old Testament.

By the time of Jesus, Jerusalem was the paramount centre of the Jewish religion, and had become the archetype of the city of God. This was largely because of the presence of the Temple, a sacred enclosure built first by Solomon, David's son, and subsequently destroyed, rebuilt and enlarged by various Jewish rulers. Jesus is recorded visiting the city and the Temple in his infancy and his adolescence, and ultimately it became the destination for his ministry in the full knowledge that danger and death awaited him. In Luke's Gospel, when Jesus is warned that the supporters of King Herod are seeking his death, he replies, 'I must go on my way today and tomorrow and the day following, for it cannot be that a prophet should perish away from Jerusalem. O Jerusalem, Jerusalem, the city that kills the prophets and stones those who are sent to it!' (Luke 13.33, 34).

Jesus visits Jerusalem on the first day of the last week of his life – Holy Week – and although he retreats on a couple of occasions back to his friends at Bethany, his focus and presence are entirely centred on Jerusalem itself. Here he will meet his destiny, and here the drama of the Passion in played out. The Garden of Gethsemane in Jerusalem is where he is arrested, and he is tried in various palaces and residences of the city before being taken outside the walls to be crucified.

II

Jerusalem has been almost continuously occupied since 3000 BC. This makes it one of the most ancient cities in the world, bearing witness to a five-thousand-year history. Since its capture by King David, and its establishment as the capital of the Jewish people, it has been completely destroyed on at least two occasions, after the Babylonian invasion of 587 BC, and at the Roman suppression of the Jewish rebellion of 135 AD, when the emperor Hadrian attempted to obliterate it, establishing instead the Roman colony of Aelia Capitolina.

While Jerusalem has survived all attempts at destruction, it has been fought over for almost all of its known history. The Egyptians, Assyrians, Babylonians, Macedonians, Seleucids, Romans, Arabs, Crusaders, Turks, British, Israelis, Palestinians and Syrians have all staked their claim to this ancient place.

Yet while continually fought over, it has become a city venerated by three monotheistic world religions. For Judaism, it is the City of David and the chosen city of God; for Christianity, the place of the death and resurrection of Jesus; and for Islam, the site of Muhammed's journey into heaven, and the direction in which he ordered all Muslims to pray, before he reoriented Islam towards Mecca.

III

This history gives Jerusalem a unique significance. In the medieval world, it became the centre of the world, and legend was piled upon legend. Calvary became not just the centre of the world's redemption, but literally the centre of any map of the world, the bullseye at the heart of the globe. It was not just the site of the crucifixion and resurrection, but the place of the burial of Adam, so that Golgotha, the place of the skull, was seen as the resting place of Adam's bones. If you look at any map of the world produced in medieval Europe, the world is round (It is a myth that the medievals thought that the world was flat) but Jerusalem is at its very centre, with the three then-known continents, Europe, Africa and Asia spreading away from it.

Pilgrimage to Jerusalem became one of the most coveted journeys for the medieval Christian, and it was to secure access for pilgrims that the Crusades were begun. In some medieval cathedrals, a labyrinth was set out in the floor. This was a single path, unlike a maze, which circled round and around until the person who walked it came at last to the centre and to Jerusalem. The labyrinth was a substitute for those who could not afford pilgrimage to the earthly city, but it also became a symbol of the journey that all Christians made towards a heavenly home. In the Letter to the Hebrews (chapters 11 and 12) the writer already refers to the journey of faith as a journey to the heavenly Jerusalem, the eternal dwelling place that God has prepared for us. By the time that the last book of the New Testament (Revelation) is written, the heavenly Jerusalem comes down from God as the bride which is the fulfilment of all God's promises.

Many early maps showed Jerusalem as a round city at the centre of a round Earth, as in the picture at the head of this chapter, a version of the famous Uppsala Map from the twelfth century. In this intriguing miniature, it is possible to make out the buildings to which the pilgrim headed, the Temple (the Mosque of Omar) at the top, the mount of Calvary and the Church of the Resurrection to the bottom left, with the Tower of David and the site of the Last Supper to the bottom right.

IV

Pilgrims to Jerusalem tend to divide between those who delight in the possible historic significance of the sites, and those for whom centuries of devotion and embellishment obscure their link with the stories of the Bible. All visitors, however, become aware that Christians, Jews and Muslims compete for the same place, not always peacefully, revealing religion both at its best and worst.

As Christians, we can both mourn over the present divided city of Jerusalem and place our hope in the heavenly Jerusalem which is to come. The psalmist wrote that we should 'pray for the peace of Jerusalem! May they be secure who love you! Peace be within your walls and security within your towers!' (Psalm 122.6,7). It is often said that all roads to peace in the Middle East pass through Jerusalem, and a solution to the ownership of this city and access to it will determine relations between Israel and the Arab nations.

Christians must also look to eternity, 'for here we have no lasting city, but we seek the city that is to come' (Hebrews 13.14). Jerusalem is a symbol of the hope of heaven, and our journey until we come home to God. St Augustine wrote, 'Our hearts are restless until they find their rest in you', and Jesus promised, 'In my Father's house are many rooms. If it were not so, would I have told you that I go to prepare a place for you?' (John 14.2).

As we reflect on Jerusalem, the city that is now, and not yet come, let us pray that God would help us hold the tension between seeking peace for all on this Earth, and placing our hope in the peace to come, which is the promise of eternal life.

Lord God, we pray for the peace of Jerusalem. May the earthly city become a place of reconciliation rather than rivalry, and of peace between different peoples of race and religion. Help us also to lift our eyes to the hope of heaven, and set our feet safely on the path to the heavenly Jerusalem. Amen.

SIX

THE FOAL OF A DONKEY

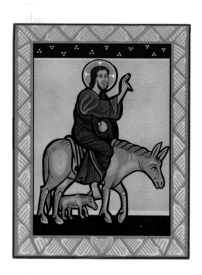

Traditionally the story of the passion kicks off with the formal entry of Jesus, riding on a donkey, into Jerusalem to be welcomed as Messiah. This is an event commemorated to this day by Christians on Palm Sunday, as palms are blessed in memory of that first entrance.

I

This event can properly be described as a formal entry, because Jesus consciously and deliberately orchestrates his entrance based upon a prophecy of Zechariah, and possible links to one of the psalms. Zechariah wrote that when the Messiah, God's chosen Saviour, arrived at Jerusalem, he would come riding on a donkey: 'Behold, your king is coming to you; righteous and having salvation is he, humble and mounted on a donkey, on a colt, the foal of a donkey' (Zechariah 9.9). Many of the psalms in the Old Testament speak of pilgrimage to Jerusalem as one of the chief goals of religious experience (cf. Psalm 122), and of the Temple as a place of worship and refuge. Although the translation is at times difficult, Psalm 118 in particular seems to speak directly into this occasion, where the crowds going up to worship cry out, 'Blessed is he who comes in the name of the Lord', and, in some translations, approach the altar in the Temple bearing branches, in the same way that the local population stripped palms from the trees for Jesus.

All these things come to pass in the account of Jesus' triumphant entry into Jerusalem. In Matthew and Luke, Jesus has arranged for a donkey to be provided to fulfil the prophecy (Matthew 21.1–7), and the crowds spread both clothes and branches to welcome Jesus. They shout 'Hosanna', a Hebrew cry that means 'Save us, we pray!', rather like Psalm 118.25, and 'Blessed is he who comes in the name of the Lord!' (Psalm 118.26). John specifically adds that the crowd was influenced by the news of the miraculous raising of Lazarus from the dead, so that Jesus is greeted as God's chosen King and Messiah.

II

Jesus wishes to leave no doubt: he is arriving in Jerusalem as the King long predicted, and he puts himself on a headlong collision course with both the Judean and the Roman authorities. John records the exasperation of the Pharisees with the situation, and, in Luke's account, they try to silence the jubilant cries of the crowd. In Matthew's account, the excitement goes on for days, with children caught up in the adventure, running around in the Temple courts and repeating the cries of hosanna. No wonder that there are side references in the Gospels to an 'insurrection'.

All this fits with what we know about Jerusalem at this time. It was a powder keg of differing political and religious parties. Jewish nationalist resistance to the Roman occupation was seething, and the Judaeans had divided into several sects and competing parties. In approaching Jerusalem from Bethany, Jesus would have arrived on the east side of the city, riding into Jerusalem through the Golden Gate, a gate traditionally associated with the arrival of the Messiah. The gate survives in Jerusalem to this day, although it has been walled up on and off since the ninth century. It was last closed by the Ottoman Sultan Suleiman the Magnificent in 1541, reportedly to ensure that no false Messiah should enter through it. For Christians, this is ironic, since we believe that Messiah had already entered through the gate one and a half millennia earlier, even if there is also a tradition that Jesus will enter Jerusalem through the same gate at the Last Judgement.

III

The donkey's sacred vocation to bear Jesus is said to be represented by a dorsal cross which is found on all donkeys to this day. It is a cross of dark skin and hair that starts between the ears and continues to the tail, with a lateral mark at the shoulders, and is more marked in some species over others. This, legend says, was imposed by God as a symbol of the donkey's readiness to share in the burden of carrying Christ towards his cross.

One of the most curious traditions arising from the Palm Sunday narratives, however, concerns the nature of Jesus' mount for the occasion. We have seen how a donkey was chosen as a product of prophecy, but the wording in Zechariah was found to be ambiguous. The prophet had literally announced, 'He is lowly and riding on a donkey and a colt, the foal of a donkey.' John merely simplifies the text of Zechariah to allow Jesus to find a colt, while Mark and Luke add the extra detail that Jesus' mount has never been ridden upon before in order to align with Zechariah's words. Matthew, however, sticks closely to the original prophecy, and both a donkey and its colt are brought for Jesus. It is not explained how Jesus sat on both, and if this seems being a little too literalistic, some of the iconographers of this scene have been imaginative in the way they depict it. My illustration is based upon an illustrated French Bible of the thirteenth century now kept in the Hague. That image charmingly shows the colt trotting faithfully between the legs of its mother so that Jesus can fulfil the prophecy in a very literal way.

IV

The sort of interplay of prophecy and fulfilment that we see in the events of Palm Sunday appears throughout the Bible. This is particularly true of the Gospel writers, who often write comments like 'This was done to fulfil the scriptures …' This raises the question of God's plan and human freedom. On occasion, as with Zechariah's prophecy, it seems that the characters of the story know the Scripture, and set out to fulfil it. More often, obscure prophecies that could only make sense after the event are chosen when those reflecting on what has happened suddenly realise that it resonates with a passage of Scripture written centuries before. Sometimes the passage of Scripture quoted appears so surprising that it seems that later writers have uncovered connections that no-one originally suspected. The more cynical might also believe that the story has been adapted in the telling to make it fit the prophecy.

If we believe that God is at work in the world, however, we should not be surprised by the idea that glimpses of God's plans can be discerned by those reflecting on God's purposes. These may only be glimpses, and sometimes may be the detection of a pattern in God's working rather than actual predictions of what must come to pass. God will always choose to work through the humble of heart and the outsider and those who act in love will know God's enabling, rather than a prophecy being someone's unavoidable destiny. From this perspective prophecy becomes more a truth-telling than an oracle of what will be.

The mystery of the Passion is that Jesus came to Jerusalem to die. All the Gospels agree that Jesus repeatedly told his disciples that this would happen. Jesus' arrival in Jerusalem is therefore a test for everyone whom he will encounter. Jesus says, 'Here I am, what do you make of me? How will you respond?', while aware that some people are so deeply invested in retaining their own power and authority that they are unlikely to repent and act against deeply ingrained patterns.

Lord Jesus, when you speak to me, through the deep convictions of my conscience or in the face of an outcast or the needy and the unlovely, help me to perceive the challenge of the moment as an opportunity to prioritise your love at work through me. Move me to repentance and faith, and help me see your hand at work in my life. Amen.

SEVEN

THE TEMPLE OF SOLOMON

Matthew, Mark and Luke describe Jesus going immediately to the Temple when he arrives in Jerusalem. There, scandalised by the traders operating in the courts of the Temple, he lays into them, driving them from its courtyards. In John's Gospel, this event is placed at the beginning of Jesus' ministry. Either then we must imagine that this episode happened twice, or that John deliberately placed it at the beginning to set the tone of his Gospel and the clash between the Messiah and the people who rejected him. All the Gospels speak plainly, however: Jesus is filled with anger in this moment. Why was the Temple so important?

Like the city of Jerusalem, the Temple assumed huge significance in the Tanach (the Jewish scriptures, known to Christians as the Old Testament), and it remains significant in the Gospels as well. In the early books of the Bible, God is peripatetic, and appears in different places at different times, even when rooted to the travelling Ark of the Covenant. It is God's chosen king, David, who decides that he will build a permanent dwelling place for God. God doesn't entirely play ball. At first he shows reluctance, and finally decides that it should be David's son Solomon who should build the sanctuary, which he blesses on its consecration by descending upon it in glory.

Thereafter the Temple becomes the only place where sacrificial worship may be offered to God, a sole meeting place between God and humanity. Even then, only one person – the High Priest – may enter into the Holy of Holies on one day a year.

In the Gospels, Jesus respects the place of the Temple, emphasising its holiness, and coming, at the climax of his ministry, to occupy its courts. There is a note of ambivalence, however. When Jesus talks about the Temple, it is not clear whether he is talking about the sanctuary or about his own body, which is also the place where God dwells. There is a shift in focus from the Temple as the dwelling place of God to the presence of God in Christ. This is given symbolic significance when, at the moment Jesus dies, the great curtain, which separated the Holy of Holies from the gaze of ordinary worshippers, is torn in two (Matthew 27.51, Mark 15.38, Luke 23.45). The way to God is opened by the tearing down of the body of Christ.

The Temple visited by Jesus was effectively a third extension of building at the site (although still called 'the Second Temple'). Solomon had completed the first Temple, usually dated by archaeologists to around 957 BC. This Temple was regarded by the writers of the scriptures as one of the wonders of the ancient world, and it survived until 587 BC, when it was destroyed by the invading Babylonian forces.

When the Persian emperor, Cyrus, allowed the Jewish peoples to return to Jerusalem from the exile imposed on them by Babylon around seventy years later, work began on reconstructing the Temple, although all accounts speak of its failure to meet the expectations of those who cherished memories of Solomon's achievements. This was the Temple that was desecrated in the second century BC by the Kings of Syria, and in 63 BC by the Roman General Pompey, who marched into the Holy of Holies, and described it as 'a vacant and empty sanctuary'.

Shortly thereafter, however, Herod the Great was given rule over the province of Judaea, and, in order to improve his credentials as a Jew, transformed the Temple by extending and beautifying it. The Holy Place was reconstructed, and a vast platform to support its courtyards was erected, which survives to this day. It was this Temple that was known to Jesus, and which was eventually destroyed by the emperors Vespasian and Titus in 70 AD, and replaced with a shrine to Jupiter by the emperor Hadrian around 135 AD.

The platform left by Herod is clearly visible today, and for many years has been the only part of the Temple to which Jews are permitted access, so that many prayers for the restoration of the Temple are offered there, and written prayers slipped between the cracks between the massive foundation stones. It has therefore been called 'the Wailing Wall' in addition to its more prosaic historical name, 'the Western Wall'.

III

The site remained sacred, becoming in due course a mosque, a Christian Church, and then a mosque again, as the vicissitudes of history played out. The exact site of the Holy of Holies of the old temple is no longer known, but many people identify it with the Dome of the Rock, a structure that houses a natural rock that rises out of the platform and beneath which is a natural cave, known as 'the Well of Souls'. All manner of traditions have attached themselves to this rock. It is said that the Ark of the Covenant rested upon it, and that it is the place where Abraham brought Isaac to be sacrificed, and Jacob had his dream of ascending and descending angels.

For Muslims, the rock bears a petrified footprint, the mark of Mohammed, who leapt onto the back of a winged horse and was carried up to heaven. It is for this reason that the Muslim Caliph al-Malik built the Dome, an octagonal building beautified by a golden dome, to protect and preserve the sacred site. When Jerusalem was conquered by the Crusaders, the Dome was confused with the Temple. Sanctuary steps were carved into the rock and an altar set upon it.

The Dome of the Rock thereby became the template for what people believed the Temple of Solomon had looked like. The Knights Templar copied the design for their churches throughout Europe, creating round and domed buildings, which reflected the stories, if not actual observation, of what the Temple looked like. The picture at the head of this chapter is one such drawing – the Dome of the Rock stands in for the Temple in a Jewish text of the fifteenth century, a copy of the Torah Commentary by the great Jewish scholar Maimonides. It was clearly illustrated by someone who knew very little about the Dome of the Rock, let alone the original Temple, and there it is octagonal, with an imagined golden dome.

IV

Today only Herod's great platform for the Temple remains, although with later buildings that have their own history and traditions built upon it. It is probably one of the most intensely holy sites in the eyes of three religions, for different reasons. For Christians, however, it is a reminder that God began the story of salvation by choosing one people, and establishing his presence and place of worship in one specific location. Christian faith is rooted in specific places, and events that have a historical background.

However, there is also an ambivalence about such places. For Jesus, his own body seems to have replaced the Temple as the sign of the presence of God, and the Christian Church is, of course, described in scripture as the Body of Christ. As Paul writes: 'Do you not know that you are God's temple and that God's Spirit dwells in you?' (1 Corinthians 3.16). We look therefore towards the presence of God making his dwelling place within us, rather than being fixed to any particular location, however holy.

It is an amazing thought, that, through Jesus' work and gift, we can each become a dwelling place for God, through which he can achieve his mission in the healing of the world.

God of our Fathers, you have called us to be your people, the temple in which the Holy Spirit dwells. Help me to be built into that spiritual Temple, to become a person through whom you can work for the redeeming of the world. Amen.

EIGHT

JUDAS ISCARIOT

The name Judas has entered the English language as the name of a traitor. However, who is this disciple of Jesus, one of the Twelve, and what is his role in the Passion of Christ?

I

Judas appears in all four Gospels as one of the Twelve, who were the closest and most trusted group of the disciples of Jesus. All the evangelists know what is going to happen, however, and Judas is described variously as untrustworthy, a thief (John 12.6) or even a devil (John 6.70). He is portrayed at several points as being out of sympathy with the actions of the others, and appears to be increasingly alienated from Jesus. It seems that while Jesus was at Bethany, Judas decided to seek out the

Temple authorities, and ask for payment to betray Jesus – the notorious thirty pieces of silver. This is why, in some traditions, the Wednesday of Holy Week is known as 'Spy Wednesday'. On the Thursday evening, Judas shows the way to the Temple guards and brings them to Jesus, identifying him from among the disciples by greeting him with a kiss. The picture at the head of this chapter is adapted from a painting of the moment of Judas' betrayal by the fourteenth-century Italian artist Ugolino de Nerio.

II

The name given to Judas, 'Iscariot', has been the subject of significant debate. Its most straightforward meaning would be to relate it to the southern Palestinian town of Kerioth, so that it means 'from Kerioth', an interpretation that fits, given that John names his father as Simon Iscariot, so sharing the same surname. Others, however, see a more sinister background. Judaism in the time of Jesus had split into several factions. The most radical of these, as described by the near contemporary Jewish historian Josephus, were the 'sicarii', the dagger men, who set themselves the task of assassinating collaborators with the Roman authorities. If 'Iscariot' is a form of 'sicarius' then it marks Judas out as among the most radical of Jesus' disciples, a dangerous man to know, and perhaps disappointed that Jesus was not agitating for the overthrow of the Romans. He is described as the keeper of the common purse of the disciples, and Jesus always seems to understand and accept his actions, even if his motives are obscure to the other disciples. According to John's Gospel, Jesus even instructs him to depart and carry out his act of betrayal (John 13.26).

III

Given the extraordinary role given to Judas in the Gospels, it is not surprising that Judas became something of a hate figure in tradition. In art, he is often shown clothed in yellow, the colour of cowardice, and a colour that became associated with people of the Jewish faith in Christian anti-Semitism.

One of the strangest traditions is found in the apocryphal Gospel of Barnabas. This Gospel recounts that Judas' appearance was changed miraculously into that of Jesus at the time of Jesus' arrest, so that Jesus was free to return to heaven, and that it was Judas, not Jesus, who was crucified on the cross. It was this tradition that made the jump into Islam, and it is recorded by the fourteenth-century Islamic scholar Al-Dimashqi. In Islam, it is inconceivable that a prophet like Jesus should have suffered the obloquy of death on a cross, so that Jesus escapes death, and for Al-Dimashqi, Judas is actually seeking to protect Jesus, and sacrifices himself in his place.

In 1970s, fragments of a Coptic manuscript were discovered, which purported to be a 'Gospel of Judas'. It appears to date from the second century AD, and it tells the story of Jesus' passion from the point of view of Judas. Intriguingly, it builds upon the hints in John's Gospel that Jesus was fully aware of Judas' plans to betray him and narrates that Judas was actually following Jesus' instructions. The text shows clear links with a branch of early Christianity known as Gnosticism, which saw the material world as evil, and the spiritual world as true and imperishable. The destruction of Jesus' body therefore only reveals his true spiritual nature. We can safely say that this text does not represent mainstream Christian faith and the early Church writer Irenaeus condemned the Gospel of Judas as heretical. However, it does address a paradox: if Jesus had to die on the cross to save the world, was Judas, by betraying Jesus, doing God's will?

IV

The New Testament tells two stories about how Judas died. In the Book of Acts, we are told that Judas bought a field (the Potter's Field) with his silver, but walking in it one day, he falls down and his stomach bursts, causing him to die. The field, we're told, is renamed 'the field of blood'. However, in Matthew's Gospel, Judas quickly repents of his act of betrayal, tries to return the pieces of silver, and then commits suicide by hanging. It is the Temple authorities who use the silver to buy the field.

How then are we to regard this figure, the betrayer of Jesus? Are we to condemn him for his treachery, or acknowledge that he will have had his motives, perhaps even being redeemed by the fact that he played his part in salvation history?

Jesus seems to have accepted and even invited Judas' role, and, in the end, I believe that Jesus will have offered Judas forgiveness for his betrayal. Judas' real sin was not in turning Jesus over to the authorities, but in his despair, 'I have sinned by betraying innocent blood' (Matthew 27.4), so that he believed he could not be forgiven and restored. With God, there is surely always a way back, and there is no sin for which Jesus did not pay the price on the cross. As the prophet Isaiah promised: 'Though your sins are like scarlet, they shall be as white as snow; though they are red like crimson, they shall become like wool' (Isaiah 1.18).

Loving God, preserve us from despair. Help us to know that there is always a way back to you through repentance and faith, and help us to extend this hope of forgiveness to all that we encounter. Amen.

NINE
ANNAS & CAIAPHAS

Once Jesus has been arrested, he is put through a series of interrogations and trials. One of his first encounters is with the High Priests, Annas and Caiaphas, before whom he is arraigned. How do these leaders of the Judaean establishment react to this potential Messiah in their midst?

I

In the Gospels according to Matthew and Mark, Jesus is taken from the Garden of Gethsemane to the house of Caiaphas the High Priest. Luke tells us that the Sanhedrin, or ruling council of the Jews, met at daybreak. Here Jesus is interrogated about his ambivalence towards the Temple, but he remains silent until directly challenged as to whether he is the Messiah. His declaration is greeted as blasphemy, and Jesus is dispatched to Pilate.

Although John's Gospel is widely believed to have been the last to be written, he often seems to have inside knowledge of the political scene in Judaea. John recounts that Jesus is first taken to Annas, who is also described as high priest, and it is Annas who sends Jesus onto his son-in-law, Caiaphas. In his account, the trial happens before Annas, and little detail is given about what happens before Caiaphas.

II

This could well reflect the historical situation. We know from sources like Josephus that Annas had held the office of High Priest between 6 and 15 AD. He was succeeded in the role first by his son, Eleazar ben Ananas, and then by his son-in-law, Joseph ben Caiaphas in 18 AD, who was installed in office by the Roman governor, Valerius Gratus, the predecessor of Pilate. Caiaphas governed the Temple as High Priest for eighteen years. Luke, at the beginning of his Gospel, and again in Acts, wrote about Annas and Caiaphas as High Priests together (Luke 3.2), and some scholars have seen this as a lack of historical knowledge. It is quite believable, however, that Annas retained some legitimacy, at least as the elder statesman, and we should not be surprised to see him still taking an active role in affairs, a role that he continues to exercise with Caiaphas in the Book of Acts.

It has already been noted how Judaism in the time of Jesus has split into various factions, and we have been introduced to the Sicarii. One of the major factions, the Sadducees, formed a sort of aristocracy for Judaea. They were a group of families who held power through the priesthood and control of the Temple. The Sadducees were conservative in outlook and had not embraced some of the newer ideas in Jewish thought, like the resurrection from the dead and the possibility of an afterlife. As people of wealth and power, they were compromised by their connections with the Romans. They were roundly condemned by groups like the Zealots, who sought the destruction of Roman power, and even the Pharisees, who were a far humbler group, who studied the Jewish Torah, the Law, and emphasised that Jews should keep themselves apart and pure from foreign influences. As Sadducees, Annas and Caiaphas were probably looked upon with suspicion, but there are hints of connections between the Sadducees and the disciples, as we shall see.

It is the High Priest Caiaphas who decides that Jesus should suffer the death penalty. Exasperated by rumours of miracles like the raising of Lazarus, and later by the occupation of the Temple by the supporters of Jesus, Caiaphas is also mindful of the danger to his own power base if his reputation is compromised with the Romans. The eleventh chapter of John's Gospel recounts the story. As the Jewish rulers discuss what is happening, it is Caiaphas who makes the expedient choice: 'It is better for you that one man should die for the people, not that the whole nation should perish' (John 11.50).

III

This leads us into one of the darkest chapters of Christianity: the Blood Libel. There is no doubt in the Gospels that the Jewish authorities decided that Jesus was a threat to their power and that he should be eliminated. After the death of Jesus, however, relations between the emerging Christian community and the religious communities of the Jews remained fraught. It is hardly surprising. At first, the Jews were the larger community, and frequently took the lead in ostracising the new Christians. However, since Christianity was open to both Jew and Gentile, it quickly became the larger faith. Increasingly, the bitterness that some Christians felt towards Judaism erupted into open hatred, and just a few centuries after the lives of the apostles, it was Christians who were persecuting the Jews.

In Matthew's account of the trial before Pilate, the crowds, whipped up against Jesus make a fateful declaration: 'His blood be on us and on our children' (Matthew 27.25). Now, it might be argued that the blood of Jesus brings blessing. As the blood of the paschal lamb at the Passover protected the people of Israel, so the blood of Jesus brings forgiveness. Sadly, not all Christians have seen it that way, however, and a stream of Christian theology went out of its way to blame the Jews for killing the Son of God. It should be a source of great shame for Christians that some of our greatest theologians, people like St John Chrysostom and Martin Luther, have issued some of the greatest calumnies against the Jewish people. This has often led to vindicative assaults against the Jewish community, pogroms and persecutions. Crowds would unexpectedly turn against the Jews living in their midst, and, as in York in 1190, massacre hundreds. It culminated in the most awful crime of all, the Jewish Holocaust in Nazi Germany and other countries, when between five and six million Jews were murdered for no crime but being Jewish.

It is true that the Nazis were hardly Christian, but it is also true that Christians created the legacy that made it so easy for Hitler to direct his wrath at the Jewish community. It should be a ground for repentance for Christians, and a warning of what religious intolerance can do.

IV

The picture on which I based my illustration of Annas and Caiaphas is a twelfth-century fresco at the Mirozhsky Monastery at Pskov in Russia. It shows two teachers of the law in dress that is appropriately Jewish. There is one detail of the original, however, that I could not bring myself to reproduce. Both priests are shown as physically blind. It might be argued that only symbolism is intended, depicting the fact that Annas and Caiaphas could not recognise Jesus as Messiah. But such symbolism, however well intended, plays into the script of anti-Semitism.

How should Christians approach Judaism and other religions? We must always beware of the dangers of extremism, of claiming superiority. I was taught by a wise scholar that the hallmarks of Christian relations with other religions should be characterised by the attitudes of Jesus himself – generosity and hospitality.

When we listen to others talk about their faith, we should always practise generosity and look for the most positive interpretation and what we can affirm, rather than approach another's faith with a critical spirit. Just look at how Jesus handles the woman at the well (John 4) or the Syrophoenician woman (Mark 6, which starts badly but quickly improves). So too, Christians, like Jews, are invited to offer hospitality (Leviticus 19.34 and Hebrews 13.2). As Christ has welcomed us, so we ought to welcome those who need our protection and help. It is a healthy counterpoint to the intolerance that can so easily take root among us, if we give in to fear of the stranger.

Lord Jesus Christ, you suffered at the hands of your own people, and yet their rejection was only the rejection that humanity offers so often of the call to holiness. Help us to be people of generosity and hospitality, offering respect and ready to learn from unexpected places. Amen.

TEN
PONTIUS PILATE

I remember a cartoon from many years back: Pilate, looking worried, is talking to his wife, and she is replying to him, 'Don't worry, dear, very few people will actually be named in the Apostle's Creed.' The joke, of course, is that only two people are named – Jesus himself, and in the phrase 'who suffered under Pontius Pilate', Pilate himself. Why is this name so significant?

I

Immediately after his trials before the Jewish authorities, Jesus is packed off to the Roman governor, with a formal request for his sentencing. In differing ways, the four Gospel writers depict the trial before Pontius Pilate as a tussle about authority.

It almost seems that no-one wants to take the final decision, and responsibility for the condemnation of Jesus is passed to and fro between the High Priests, the wider Jewish leadership, the Roman Governor and Herod. This macabre 'pass the parcel' even takes place between Jesus himself and Pilate, as they appear to trade questions about the nature of kingship and truth. Pilate seems to do everything he can to avoid condemning Jesus, offering the crowds a choice of prisoners to release, trying to make do with a flogging as opposed to a crucifixion, and finally, creating one of the most famous of metaphors, literally washing his hands of the situation.

II

Historically, the evidence for Pilate's tenure as Prefect of the Roman Province of Judaea, Samaria and Idumaea – the former Kingdom of Herod the Great – is well founded. He appears not only in the four Gospels but in the near contemporary histories of Josephus and Tacitus, and in the writings of Philo of Alexandria, one of the leading Jewish philosophers. The role of Prefect was basically that of a military commander charged with keeping the peace, assisted by a garrison of about 3000 troops. The emperor Tiberius appointed Pilate to the role, and he stayed in it for longer than the usual term of office – for ten years, beginning in 26 AD. His career went nowhere, and he is said to have died in 37 AD.

The capital of the Roman administration was not at Jerusalem, but the Roman port of Caesarea Maritima, where in 1961 an excavation found an inscription that named him. From there, Pilate would have to travel up to the Roman garrison fortress of Antonia, which overlooked Jerusalem.

The Gospels correctly portray Pilate as making the final decision about crucifixion. In a Roman province the power to execute offenders was taken from local authorities, and the High Priests would have had to ask for the ultimate penalty from the Roman Governor. This political role is demonstrated by the demands made of Pilate to execute Jesus, coupled with a threat that a failure to do so would be an act of treason against Caesar. The Jewish authorities were playing a canny game of political manipulation.

III

In tradition, several places were designated as the birthplace of Pilate: Bisenti in Italy, Tarragona in Spain, and, rather unexpectedly, Fortingall in Scotland. Likewise, it is said by some that he died at Mount Pilatus in Switzerland, and some say his ghost still haunts the mountain. Others say he committed suicide in Vienne near Lyon in France, or in Rome, perhaps at the order of the emperor Caligula. The Ethiopian Orthodox Church have made him a saint, and tell stories of his conversion.

In the picture attached to this chapter, Pilate is shown as a Byzantine Roman Governor with all the panoply of official purple robes and staff of office. It is adapted from a mosaic of the trial of Jesus in the Basilica of Saint Mark in Venice, and shows a careworn, perhaps even sympathetic character.

IV

There is no reason to feel any sympathy for Pilate. His reputation was of a brutal man, and a particularly violent episode, when he massacred Samaritan protestors, seems to have caused his recall to Rome at the end of his decade of service. Pilate is shown as a prevaricator in the Gospels. Some say that this is because the evangelists were anxious to depict

Rome as less responsible for the death of Jesus, but it strikes me as the cynical act of a politically minded civil servant, who prefers others to take the risks of decision.

In particular, there seems to be a contrast at the trials of Jesus between Pilate, who cannot distinguish truth from political expediency – 'What is truth?' he snaps at Jesus at one point in the trial, when Jesus speaks of his mission to speak God's truth – and Jesus, who is patient and calm before his judge, and behaves with a natural authority.

Lord Acton, the English Catholic historian and politician, is well known for writing 'Power tends to corrupt, and absolute power corrupts absolutely. Great men are almost always bad men ...' We might not wish to be so certain in our own judgement, but still acknowledge that the taste of power can sharpen an inner conflict between doing what is right and doing what is necessary to maintain power. We should pray for all those who hold power in this world, a power that Jesus challenged when he said that those who wished to be first in the Kingdom of God should be the servant of all (Mark 10.44).

Lord God, source of true power and wisdom, we pray for all those who hold power in this world. Keep them anchored to their humanity and empathy with others, and steer them always into the path of righteous humility and away from the perils and addictions of authority. Amen.

ELEVEN

CLAUDIA PROCULA

If ever there was a minor character in Scripture, Claudia Procula is the one. Even her name is not recorded in Scripture, and she appears in one verse in one Gospel only. Who is Claudia Procula, and what does she add to the story of the passion?

I

In the four accounts of the trials of Jesus, only one – Matthew – makes mention that Pilate's wife, who is not named, sends the Prefect a message in the course of Jesus' trial: 'Have nothing to do with that righteous man, for I have suffered much because of him today in a dream' (Matthew 27.19). There is little context and no details of the dream. However, it is cited by the evangelist as evidence why Pilate acted cautiously in response to the demands for the death of Jesus. The description of Jesus as a righteous man is also intriguing – has Pilate's wife heard from the circle of aristocratic wives that Jesus is on the side of the angels? There are hints that the circle around Jesus reached into high places – Peter gets entry into the High Priest's home because the disciple accompanying him (Is it John?) is known personally to the High Priest (John 18.15), while the steward of King Herod Antipas has a wife, Joanna, who is one of the financial backers of Jesus and his disciples (Luke 8.3). We have no idea where Matthew learned the intriguing morsel of information, which is unknown elsewhere.

II

It is almost certain that Pilate was married – almost all Roman aristocrats were – and by the reign of the emperor Tiberius wives could accompany their husbands on their tours of duty, so it is entirely possible that this narrative is historically accurate. Pilate's wife acquires her name in the apocryphal writings of the third century or thereabouts: first a family name – Procla or Procula – and then a first name, Claudia. Again, these are common names in the ancient world, witnessed by the existence of several tombs of women bearing exactly the same name from these early centuries. This is not enough evidence for a connection, however, even if one scholar has linked the wife of Pilate to the Claudia mentioned by the apostle Paul in 2 Timothy 4.21.

The picture I have assigned to Claudia is adapted from a funeral portrait of an anonymous burial in the Faiyum in Egypt from the third century. At this stage, mummified remains were often prepared with remarkably lifelike portraits painted in wax and attached as a death mask, and this illustration reflects a beautifully realistic portrait of an aristocratic lady from those times.

III

In the Eastern Churches Claudia becomes St Procla, and in the Gospel of Nicodemus, also with its appendix known as the Acts of Pilate, both she and Pilate mourn the death of Jesus. Tradition goes on to make them both saints, living lives of exemplary holiness and charity.

Christian writers were more divided about the significance of her dream, however. For St Augustine and St Jerome, and even John Calvin, the dream was sent from God, the divine truth about Jesus being imparted by revelation. St Bede and St Bernard of Clairvaux with Martin Luther, however, describe the dream as coming from Satan, sent to place obstacles in the path of the story of salvation, distracting Pilate, and seeking to prevent the sacrificial death of the Messiah.

IV

What strikes me are the very human dimensions of the story. Pilate becomes a more nuanced character as we realise that he was a man with a family, and those near and dear to him who could influence his thinking. We sometimes forget that the story of Jesus is embedded in real humanity, where the motives and thinking of individuals are rarely solitary, but influenced by their background, family and friends.

We tend to do the same thing with the people who appear in our news and in our press. We neglect their humanity, and turn them into cardboard cut outs of villains or heroes, one dimensional characters whom we can co-opt into our understanding of good and evil. Our spouses and partners, too, if we have them, are often humanising influences on us, rounding out our characters, and helping us to think more deeply about the daily transactions of life and work. Claudia

Procula humanises Pilate, and reminds us not to rush to judgement; not to see individual human beings as wholly bad or good. 'No man is an island', the poet John Donne wrote.

As we reflect on Claudia Procula, let us remember the complexity of the relationships that help to make us who we are. Friends and family members soften us, and shape us through their love or companionship. Let us pray that we shall be slow to judge anyone, and remember there are more sides to their story than the interaction that we witness or find most obvious.

Lord God, each of us is a wonderful creation, but shaped by many interactions. Help us to tread softly when we make judgements about others, and realise that there are facets of other people that we might never see that redeem and make holy even those who strike us as made ugly by their misdeeds. Amen.

TWELVE

BARABBAS

If Matthew alone mentions Pilate's wife, all four Gospels mention another character who is influential in the course of Jesus' trial: the bandit Barabbas. What part does this character play in the passion of Jesus?

I

We have already noticed the reluctance of Pilate to sentence Jesus to death. In the Gospels, one of the ways in which Pilate seeks to avoid the inevitable is by invoking what has been called 'the Paschal Privilege'. All four Gospels bear witness to a tradition by which one prisoner can be released from penalty as a mark of respect for the Jewish festival. Pilate invites the crowd to choose between Jesus and Barabbas. In Matthew, Barabbas is a notorious criminal, while in Mark, he is someone who has committed murder in the insurrection, and was imprisoned with 'the rebels'. (Is this an echo of the events of Palm Sunday being rather more violent than we tend to believe?) Barabbas has a similar record in Luke's Gospel, although the reference to the insurrection is rather more vague, and the suggestion for his release comes not from Pilate, but from the crowd. In John, Pilate introduces the custom of the Paschal Privilege as a right of the people, and proposes to release 'the King of the Jews'. As in Luke, it is the crowd that propose Barabbas, although here he is described as a robber.

II

In historical records outside the Bible, there is no mention of the Paschal Privilege, and this has led some scholars to conclude that it was an invention and a device to let Pilate off the hook, and to implicate the Jewish people. Certainly, it seems rather unlike the Pilate of history to show such clemency. The fact that the story appears in all four Gospels, however, and without commentary, suggests that it was an early and widely attested element in the story of the trial of Jesus. Modern commentators, including Pope Benedict XVI, have tried to distinguish between the whole of the Jewish people and the specific crowds named. They should be limited to the religious leaders and possibly the supporters of Barabbas. Certainly, they seem a different crowd from the pilgrims and visitors to Jerusalem for the festival who made up the crowds entering Jerusalem with Jesus on Palm Sunday.

The parallel between the two prisoners offered by Pilate is highlighted by some of the variants of the early Greek manuscripts of the New Testament. *Bar Abbas* means 'the Son of the Father', or possibly, *Bar Rabban*, 'the Son of the

Teacher'. In some early manuscripts of Matthew's Gospel, the parallel is even more heightened, since Barabbas is given a first name, Jesus. In these manuscripts, Pilate cries out, 'Whom do you want me to release for you, Jesus, the Son of the Father, or Jesus who is called the Christ?' (Matthew 27.17).

III

The crowds are best understood as representing the whole of humanity, rather than one section of it. The point that the evangelists are making is the contrast between the innocent Messiah, whom we are prepared to crucify, and the blood-stained bandit, whom political expediency encourages us to let off. It is easier to put up with the mediocrity of sin than to face the challenging call of holiness.

Barabbas drops out of sight in the Scriptures after he has played his part. Nor does Christian tradition make much of him. It is only when modern ideas of psychology develop that people begin to speculate on what it was like for this criminal facing death to have been pardoned in the place of Christ. In 1950, the Swedish author Pär Lagerkvist wrote a novel called *Barabbas* in which he explored the psychology of the bandit, who has never experienced love and struggles to make sense of the Christian story of Jesus, witnessing the crucifixion, and interrogating the disciples to discover their understanding of what Jesus did. Ultimately, he is sentenced for his ongoing crimes, and surrenders himself to a pointless death uncomprehending of the power of love. This rather relentless novel was adapted into a Hollywood film in 1961, starring Anthony Quinn as Barabbas, a photo of which I drew upon for the picture in this chapter. In the film, Barabbas finds redemption, befriending a Christian and encountering Peter in Rome, before finding faith at the last.

IV

For me, the focus of the story lies not in the choice of the crowd, but in the fact that Jesus dies in the place of Barabbas. He finds freedom as Jesus goes to death in his place. From this point of view, we are all of us Barabbas, in whose place Jesus has died.

One of the great Christian words is 'redemption', which signifies the manner in which Jesus buys us from the futility of sin, purchasing us with his blood to free us for a new life of holiness and love. As I argued in the first chapter of this book, the emphasis here should not be on the punishment, but on the purchase, as God pays the price to release us for a better life. Unlike the pointlessness of Lagerkvist's *Barabbas*, we are let go into a new life, with the promise of the Spirit to empower us for the task of sharing in Christ's mission. As Paul wrote in his letter to the Romans: 'The wages of sin is death, but the free gift of God is eternal life in Christ Jesus our Lord' (Romans 6.23). It is a wonderful exchange. The seventeenth-century Anglican priest and hymn writer Samuel Crossman expressed the idea well in the hymn 'My Song is Love Unknown':

> They rise and needs will have
> My dear Lord made away;
> A murderer they save,
> The Prince of Life they slay.
> Yet cheerful he
> To suffering goes,
> That he his foes
> From thence might free.

THIRTEEN
SIMON OF CYRENE

Another of the 'supporting cast' in the story of Jesus' Passion is Simon of Cyrene. His appearance in Scripture is also brief, as he is compelled to assist Jesus on the walk to Golgotha, the site of the crucifixion. Who is Simon, and what is his significance?

I

Matthew, Mark and Luke – but not John – all recount, almost in passing, that as Jesus was taken to be crucified, the Roman soldiers compelled a man from Cyrene, Simon, to carry the cross of Jesus. Mark and Luke add the detail that Simon was travelling into Jerusalem from the country, but Mark included a different piece of information, which tantalises. Simon, he writes, is the father of Alexander and Rufus. The fact that all three evangelists name Simon suggests that he might be a figure well-known to the early Church, and it demonstrates the closely woven nature of the early Christian community. The earliest readers were presumably also expected to know the Alexander and Rufus to whom Mark makes reference. There are both an Alexander and a Rufus elsewhere in the New Testament. In Acts 19, there is an Alexander who is a leading Jew in Ephesus, and in 1 Timothy, Paul speaks of a former colleague, Alexander, with whom he has fallen out. Rufus is identified as a member of the early Roman Church, in Paul's Letter to the Romans (16.13), together with his mother, of whom Paul has fond memories. Of course, such names were commonplace, and there is no good evidence of a link, but I like to think, at least, that perhaps the Rufus living in Rome with his mother was well known as the son of Simon.

II

Cyrene was a major city founded by the Greeks on the north coast of what is today Libya, with a large Jewish population. We may assume that Simon was one of those members of the Jewish community who had made the long trek to visit Jerusalem for the Passover and related festivals. At Pentecost, a few weeks later, Jews from Cyrene are listed among those in the Book of Acts who listen to the disciples speaking in their own language. Travel, especially for business or religion, was much more widely spread in the ancient world than we tend to assume from all the difficulties of journeying.

It doesn't feel too big a jump to portray Simon as of African descent. The icon on which I have based the picture in this chapter is a modern one, produced by an anonymous American artist, which depicts Simon as being Black. Interestingly, the famous Black actor Sidney Poitier was chosen to play the part in the Hollywood film *The Greatest Story Ever Told*.

III

St Francis in the thirteenth century developed a deep love of the Holy Land, and founded a specific province for his Order, the Friars Minor, who were dedicated to protecting the holy sites and welcoming pilgrims to the city. By the fourteenth century, they were offering guided tours of the 'Via Dolorosa', a route winding through the streets of Jerusalem, purporting to be the route by which Jesus travelled from the Roman fortress of Antonia to the site of Calvary. A series of shrines were built, where people could stop and pray in relation to the various episodes of Jesus' last journey, and the fifth station was dedicated to Simon of Cyrene. By the eighteenth century, churches all over the Christian world were erecting sets of Stations of the Cross in their Churches, and Simon became an important part of this devotional cycle.

Although Simon had been compelled to carry Jesus' cross, Simon very quickly came to be seen as a companion who came to the rescue of Jesus in his suffering, and therefore as the archetype of the person who comes to assist those in need. Two modern Christian organisations that help the homeless take their inspiration from him – the Simon Community and the Cyrenians, whose origins are linked but who operate to this day in the UK and Ireland.

IV

Simon's action can therefore be seen as a beautiful example of companionship. He comes alongside Jesus at a time of great need, and assists in bearing the weight of the cross. Sometimes when we are in the greatest need, God will send a Simon to come alongside us, and to assist in carrying our burdens.

Here lies the relevance of Simon for us all. None of us is freed from the burdens of life simply because we are people of faith. However, we can look for God to send us those who will walk alongside us. If discipleship is the task of 'taking up our own cross' (Luke 9.23), then we should pray that there will be those whom God sends us to be with us in carrying the burden, just as we should be ready to come alongside others to help them in their difficulties. Friendship and companionship are huge sources of strength and comfort in the path of life, and Simon's example provides both inspiration and hope.

Let us reflect upon those who have been for us like Simon of Cyrene, and perhaps recall those whom we have been able to come alongside.

Lord God, who gave Simon of Cyrene to be a companion to Jesus, and to assist him in carrying the weight of the cross, help us, at all times, to be ready to join others who suffer, and give us the grace of companionship in our hour of need. Amen.

FOURTEEN
VERONICA

If Simon of Cyrene was chosen by the Franciscans for the Fifth Station of the 'Via Dolorosa', then they delved deep into the legends of the crucifixion for the Sixth Station.

I

The evangelist Luke describes another encounter by Jesus on the walk to Calvary. Luke records that Jesus was followed by a huge crowd, including women, who may well have been disciples, as the evangelist records them as weeping for Jesus. Although the women of Jerusalem are allotted their own station (Number 8), it is possible that the events described as involving the woman called Veronica may have happened in some shape or form – a gentle act of wiping our Lord's face in the midst of the pull and shove of the crowds.

The legend of Veronica, however, goes a great deal further. Veronica shows mercy to Jesus by seeking to wipe his brow, and this act of mercy is rewarded with a miracle. The imprint of Christ's face is left on the veil that she uses.

It is hard to know how this legend began. From the early centuries, people were curious about the appearance of Christ and as early as the fourth century, records appear of enquiries being made as to the likeness of Jesus. Images of the face of Jesus only begin to be produced after 'the Peace of the Church', when the emperor Constantine abolished the persecution of Christianity and gave it official status in the Empire. The earliest images show Jesus as a youthful clean-shaven shepherd, but by the fifth century, the image that we recognise now, of a bearded, long-haired Christ begins to dominate.

By the eleventh century, images of Christ's face begin to be depicted in connection with the crucifixion, and the Lord's face begins to be represented with the crown of thorns and drops of blood. By the thirteenth century, medieval meditations on the life of Christ begin to include the legend of Veronica in the form we know it, and speak of the creation of a miraculous image of Christ's face.

Alongside this tradition, there are references to a relic known as the Mandylion, which purported to be a portrait of Jesus from life gifted to King Abgar of Edessa. Throughout the medieval world, images described as the Mandylion, or as the Veil of Veronica, multiply, and with them a claim to authenticity, citing their possible miraculous origin. Even Veronica's name appears to be a play on the Latin, *vera icona*, 'the true image', rather than any historical name. One such relic in particular, preserved in Rome, drew pilgrims from the twelfth century on.

All these legends are so late, it is difficult to think they have any historical foundation, but there is one possibility, which centres on the history of a relic known as the Shroud of Turin. Today, the Shroud is based in the Cathedral in Turin, and is a sheet over four metres in length bearing both a front and reverse image of the body of Jesus. Historically, this can only be dated back as far as the fourteenth century, but some researchers have suggested that when folded to show only the face, it matches descriptions given of the Mandylion or the veil. Might this mysterious image be responsible for both the legend of Edessa's image, and the veil of Veronica?

IV

The image I have produced for this chapter is based upon a modern copy of an icon of Veronica preserved on Mount Athos, the collection of great Orthodox monasteries isolated on the Athos peninsula in northern Greece. It demonstrates how far Christianity has come from its parent faith, Judaism, by allowing the depiction of images with divine status.

In the Bible, the second commandment forbids the production of images of God, and a persistent battle with idols is a feature of the Old Testament. Islam inherited this aversion to images of holy men, and even Mohammed, the prophet of Islam, is never pictured, except with a veil covering his face.

In the eighth and ninth centuries in eastern Christianity, Christians erupted into violent conflict about whether it was right to have images of Jesus and the saints. In the West, a similar controversy played a significant part in the Reformation, when many medieval images were destroyed. Despite such violent upheavals, however, Christianity tends to be comfortable with images of Jesus, so long as the offering of worship to those images is avoided.

Why? There is an important truth to Christianity about the image of God in contrast to the other Abrahamic faiths. We believe that God was in Jesus reconciling the world to himself (2 Corinthians 5.19), and that 'he is the radiance of God's glory and the exact imprint of his nature' (Hebrews 1.3). Since God has been incarnate and lived as a man, it became permissible to depict him. Although no image now – with the possible exception of the Shroud or a Veil of Veronica – claims to be an exact representation of the face of Jesus, images of Jesus reflect his human incarnation and bear quiet witness to the truth that Christ, for Christians, is fully God and fully man.

Lord Jesus, you are the Lord, our God incarnate, and the living One. Help us to bear the image of your love in our lives, and allow the image of God to be seen through our service. Amen.

FIFTEEN

GESTAS & DISMAS

Christ was not alone in being crucified on Good Friday. Who else suffered in the same way, and what was their story?

I

Matthew and Mark record that two rebels – were they part of the same insurrection as Barabbas? – were crucified on either side of Jesus. John mentions two others being crucified with Jesus, as he tells the story of how the soldiers came to break the legs of the crucified – a gesture, as we will see, of cruel significance. Luke records a longer story. He confirms what the other evangelists write, that Jesus was crucified between two others, although Luke names them as criminals rather than rebels. However, Luke includes the extra details that one of the criminals shouted insults at Jesus, goading Jesus that he should have saved the three of them if he was the promised Messiah.

The other, it is recorded, rebuked the first, however, speaking of the innocence of Christ in contrast to their own guilt. It is this second criminal who then turns to Jesus in a confession of faith: 'Jesus, remember me when you come into your kingdom' (Luke 23.42). In response, the Lord makes a promise, 'Truly, I say to you, today you will be with me in paradise' (Luke 23.43).

II

Crucifixion was used by the Romans as a particularly horrendous punishment, often reserved for slaves or for those who had rebelled against Roman rule. Although it was seen as particularly severe, and described by the Roman writer Cicero as 'a most cruel and disgusting punishment', it was widely used. In the first century BC, following the defeat of the rebellion of Spartacus, who had led an army of slaves against the Romans, literally hundreds of the rebels were crucified along the Esquiline Way leading out of Rome.

The punishment involved stripping a person and fixing them naked to a pole or cross, which could take different shapes, or even impaling them upon it, and leaving them in public to die, exposed, as a warning to others. The political nature of the punishment raises again the question of how Jesus was seen by the Romans, a rebel against the power of Rome – evidenced as well by the charge written over his head 'The King of the Jews'.

Victims were then left to die for as long as it took – there are references in Roman histories of people surviving for three days or more. They would hang from the cross experiencing increasing pain from their wounds, which could lead to blood poisoning, heart failure, or finally suffocation, as the strength of those crucified failed, and they could no longer support their own bodies to breathe. This is the significance of the story, recorded in John, of soldiers being sent to break the legs of the crucified, and to hasten their death before the beginning of the festival. If the legs of those crucified were broken, they would no longer be able to haul themselves up upon the cross, in order to relieve the stress on their chests and to breathe more easily.

III

I have adapted my pictures of the two criminals crucified with Jesus from the *Hortus Deliciarum*, a religious encyclopaedia compiled in the twelfth century by Herrad, the Abbess of the monastery of Hohenburg in Alsace. Among other pictures, set out for the instruction of young novices and nuns, is a large picture of the crucifixion, including many of the characters involved.

Not surprisingly, in the centuries that followed, there was much curiosity about who the two criminals might have been. We have already noted that many gospels, or lives of Jesus, exist from the early centuries of Christianity. Only four were identified as reliable by the early Church, and included in the canon (or list) of the Scriptures. In the others that have survived, there is a great deal of speculation, which often provides details that the four Gospels omit. From these apocryphal gospels, we learn that the two crucified with Jesus were brothers, by the names of Gestas and Dismas. Eventually a whole life story was constructed for the brothers, in which the older, Gestas, leads the younger, Dismas, into a life of crime. Among their exploits was an attempt to rob Mary and Joseph as they fled into Egypt with the infant Jesus many years before. Gestas is depicted as having no compassion whatsoever, but Dismas takes pity on the family and persuades his brother to let them go. Not surprisingly, many years later, it was the compassionate Dismas who also upbraided his brother, and expressed his repentance to Jesus.

Jesus' answer, 'Today, you will be with me in paradise' (Luke 23.43), has also occasioned comment, given that his ascension into heaven comes much later. Paradise, however, in the first century did not signify heaven and the life eternal. Rather, it was one of the more pleasant regions of Sheol, the place of the dead, in which those who were counted among the righteous might await the resurrection of the dead.

IV

What is striking is the contrast between the two criminals. One, filled with anger amidst his pain, still rails that things are not working out in his favour, and is prepared to chide Jesus; the other expresses repentance, simply asking for Jesus' mercy. This is sufficient for Christ to extend to him the promise of everlasting life. I suppose that I'm reminded of Martha and Mary – one thing alone is needful, that we turn to Jesus in faith.

Almost the first words that Jesus speaks in Mark's Gospel are 'Repent, and believe in the gospel' (Mark 1.15); and repentance is no more, and no less, than turning again in the heart towards God. The Scriptures repeatedly bear witness to the fact that God is drawn towards the humble and lowly of heart, and Jesus' parable of the Pharisee and the tax-collector (Luke 18.9–14) informs us that humility before God is valued more highly than many calculated acts in fulfilment of the law.

Let us pray that God will grant us a true spirit of repentance.

Lord Jesus, as the good thief prayed that you would remember him in your kingdom, grant us true repentance of heart and mind, that turning to you, we may know your mercy, and the gift of your grace. Amen.

SIXTEEN

MARY, MOTHER OF THE LORD

Both those who had bayed for the blood of Jesus and those who stood faithfully by his side met at the foot of the cross. We are explicitly told that many of the women followers of Jesus observed the crucifixion. Among them, John tells us, was his mother.

I

Mary appears several times in the accounts of Jesus' life, often playing a crucial role. Most obviously, of course, as his mother, Mary is a central figure in the nativity narratives, but she is also there at other key moments – when Jesus is lost as a child in the Temple, at the first miracle at Cana of Galilee, at turning points of his ministry, with the Church as they embark on life after

Jesus' ascension, and here, according to John, as the foot of the cross. What takes place is quite a touching moment. Jesus sees both his mother at the foot of the cross and one of his closest disciples, John, who is described in the Gospel as 'the disciple whom he loved' (John 19.26). He greets them both – and urges them to care for one another: 'Mother, behold your son!', and to John, 'Behold your mother!' From that time, the evangelist records, the disciple took Mary into his own home.

II & III

We can only begin to grasp the grief of Mary in this scene. We know that Mary had treasured the events of the nativity (Luke 2.19) and followed the ministry of Jesus – even prompting the first miracle – although at times she seems rather worried about the direction of Jesus' ministry in a very human motherly sort of way (Mark 3.21, 31, 32). What ambitions and hopes might Mary have had for her son? If she believed that he was the Messiah, what did she expect? We know that she had been warned from the start that there was trouble in store ('A sword will pierce through your own soul also', Luke 2.35), and now she had to see her son experience the most painful and humiliating of deaths.

Christians have meditated on this scene for generations, inspiring some of the greatest music and art that the world has known. The 'Stabat Mater', a thirteenth-century hymn to Mary, attributed by some to Pope Innocent III, or alternatively to a Franciscan friar, Jacopone da Todi, has been set to music by over fifty-seven composers, including some of the world's greatest. It is a poem that calls on the suffering of Jesus' mother as a spur to our own sorrow and repentance in the light of Jesus' sacrificial death for our sakes.

Similarly, 'pietà' is an Italian name meaning 'compassion' which is used to describe any depiction of Mary mourning over the dead body of Christ as it is brought down from the cross. This is a scene that has been depicted thousands of times, but perhaps most famously by the Renaissance artist Michelangelo in a sculpture that is kept in St Peter's Basilica in Rome. My own, far humbler rendition, is an adaption of a pietà by an anonymous artist which is kept in the Basilica of St Mark in Rome.

The word 'mystery' is used in connection with Christian faith to describe those matters that will in truth always be beyond human understanding. However much we may obtain glimpses or insights into profound truth, there is always something that eludes us, and greater depths to be fathomed. The love between mother and child is in every case one such mystery – but particularly it must be the case between one who in Christian faith has been called to be the Mother of God Incarnate and her Son.

Over the centuries, this has given Mary a distinctive place in Christian art and devotion, and people have been drawn to her obvious humanity and compassion to find a saint with whom they may identify and in whom to find succour. The exuberance and enthusiasm that this has inspired in some Christians has been the subject of criticism in others, fearful that in some way a focus on Mary might eclipse a proper devotion to her son.

I do not think that we should fear the devotion offered to Mary. Her role and place in Christianity are entirely oriented around the Son who is her Saviour as much as the world's, a fact that should always be held in mind. However, Mary's place in the drama of the Passion reminds us of the very real and human dimensions of the story of salvation, and the depth of her obvious love can assist us in exploring the extent of God's love for us all.

IV

We live in a world where mothers often suffer – and fathers as well – as the result of the broken and often sinful nature of the world. Children are maimed or killed by the suicide bomber or shooter; mothers and children are displaced by war and driven into exile and refugee status. A parent will stand or sit beside a child who is ill, perhaps terminally, and undergo the torment of wishing that they could take their child's place and spare them any suffering. Heartache is the price of love in so many situations between parent and child.

Yet this also speaks of redemptive power. To be loved in times of pain and hurt is sometimes the only balm for the soul, and love binds us in mercy and compassion to the victim and sensitivity to the suffering.

The witness of Mary is that human love is drawn into the divine, and that human love and divine love are inextricably linked. 'God is love, and whoever abides in love abides in God, and God abides in them' (1 John 4.16). We should give thanks that, made in the divine image, we are creatures capable of love, and all that brings, for the meaning of life. It may bring suffering, but it also brings some of the greatest joys of life and causes of celebration. It makes us more fully human, and draws us towards God.

As we ponder the love of Mary, the Mother of the Lord, let us give thanks for love, and pray that it may be manifest in our lives.

Loving God, stir up in us the gift of love, not only for those who are near to us, but also for those who are far away, and grant to all those who love and who suffer the healing balm of the knowledge of your love, given and offered through Jesus Christ, your Son. Amen.

SEVENTEEN

LONGINUS

The soldiers who crucified Christ carried out their duties with a brutal efficiency. The centurion who led them, however, has been singled out in biblical narrative and Christian tradition for special attention.

I

In Luke's Gospel, the centurion in charge of the military detail observes the manner of Jesus' death and makes a declaration: 'Surely this was a righteous man!' (Luke 23.46). This is repeated in Mark's Gospel, although the form of the declaration is explicit in its faith: 'Truly this man was the Son of God!' (Mark 15.39). In Matthew's Gospel, we are told that the centurion was joined in his team in this same declaration, as they were disturbed by the events accompanying the moment of the death of Jesus, which included an earthquake and other signs.

John's Gospel, as ever, is slightly different. In chapter 19, verses 31–37, John includes the story of the breaking of the legs to which reference has been made earlier, but the soldiers find Jesus already dead. Suspicious at so early a death, one of the soldiers, we are told by the evangelist, pierced Jesus' side with a lance, causing blood and water to seep from his body. This may well be proof of Jesus' death, since it suggests that his lungs have filled with fluid.

II & III

Over time, these two stories merge and it is the same centurion who both thrusts the spear into Jesus' side and who is later converted. An early manuscript with a depiction of the crucifixion, held in the Laurentian Library in Florence, includes letters written out alongside the centurion holding the lance in the scene. These letters have been identified as spelling out the Greek word for lance, but they may have been misinterpreted to give a name to the centurion: Longinus. At any rate, this is the name by which the centurion becomes known in later biographies of the saints.

In legend, Longinus is reported to have suffered from weak sight, a malady that is healed by drops of Christ's blood falling from the wound as he thrusts the spear into Jesus' body, and this in turn leads to his conversion. In due course, Longinus was venerated as a saint, receiving baptism from the apostles and leaving military service in order to dedicate his life to preaching the saving acts of God in Jesus back in his homeland of Cappadocia (in present day Turkey). Pursued by Pilate, legend says that Longinus suffered martyrdom for his faith, and that his head was taken to the Governor as proof of his execution.

The lance that Longinus used was also revered as a relic. Several locations claimed to have the original lance, including Rome, Constantinople and Vienna, where it began to be used among the regalia employed at the coronations of the Holy Roman Emperors. One of the most famous stories of the afterlife of the lance occurred during the First Crusade at the end of the eleventh century. The Crusaders had managed to capture the great city of Antioch back from the invading Seljuk Turks, but then had found themselves besieged by a new Seljuk army. Dispirited and downhearted, the resolve of the Crusaders to defend the city weakened, until one of the defenders, Peter Bartholomew, claimed to receive a series of visions which directed him to the Church of St Peter. There, the chroniclers recorded that Peter, guided by visions of St Andrew, managed to uncover the hiding place of the lance of Longinus. So heartened were the Crusaders at this sign of divine favour, that they rallied and succeeded in defeating their enemies, going on to the capture of Jerusalem. Unfortunately, Peter Bartholomew became so intoxicated by his visionary powers that he insisted on relaying divine commands for the subsequent conduct of the campaign. When these commands led to defeat, his reputation, and the reputation of those who had believed him, suffered greatly.

IV

The picture that heads this chapter is based upon an icon of Longinus, painted by the seventeenth-century icon painter Fyodor Zubov, kept at the Kremlin in Moscow. Longinus became one among many soldier saints who turned from their violent ways in order to honour Jesus. Among the most famous are Sergius and Bacchus, and Alban and George, and Longinus has been enrolled among a great tradition.

There is a certain irony in their stories, as these soldier saints were often famous for turning their backs on their military profession, in order to follow the Prince of Peace, yet they remained revered and followed by soldiers, and even co-opted into crusades. Nevertheless, they themselves speak to us of God's power to redeem humanity from the ways of war to walk in peace.

As I write this book, there is war in Europe as the forces of Russia have invaded the neighbouring country of Ukraine. It is a sorry tale, made worse by the fact that certain Christian leaders have preferred to peddle a narrative that Russia's soldiers are fighting a holy war, rather than calling the leaders of the nations to repentance and the way of peace. Let us take courage from the story of Longinus to believe that God is at work to convert the hardest of hearts and lead people away from counsels of war and hatred and into the way of peace.

Lord God, the example of Longinus teaches us to renounce violence and to seek the reconciling power of your love. We pray that our hearts may be inclined to peace, and that the hearts of the violent may be turned away from harm and destruction towards healing and reconciliation. Amen.

EIGHTEEN
JOSEPH OF ARIMATHEA

All four Gospels mention Joseph of Arimathea, the man who is bold enough (and influential enough) to approach Pilate and ask for the body of Jesus to be released to him.

I

In Matthew, he is described as a rich man and a disciple of Jesus, while Mark tells us that he was a prominent member of the Council (the Sanhedrin), waiting for the Kingdom of God. Luke adds the reassurance that Joseph had not consented to the decision and actions of the council to condemn Jesus.

Joseph oversees the removal of Jesus' body from the cross, wrapping it in a linen shroud and laying it in a fresh unused rock tomb. Matthew adds the additional detail that it was the tomb that Joseph had prepared for himself. In John's account, Joseph is assisted by another council member, Nicodemus, who is also famous from his earlier encounter with Jesus, and who donates seventy-five pounds of spices to assist with Jesus' embalming.

II

In the environs of Jerusalem about a thousand rock-cut tombs have been identified. Each one consists of one or more burial chambers, with long niches cut into the sides of the tomb to accommodate interments. All of them would have been prepared for the richer sort of person who could afford their purchase and preparation.

All this speaks of the high-status links of Jesus and his disciples. Accustomed as we are of thinking of Jesus' disciples as peasant fishermen, and Jesus as the son of a poor carpenter, it appears that they had rich and powerful allies. To be laid in a rock tomb demanded significant resources, and even nobility often shared such a last resting place. The seventy-five pounds of spices provided by Nicodemus would have been very expensive, especially as we're told by the evangelist that they were a mix of myrrh and aloes, the cost of which in contemporary values runs into six figures!

The picture I have adapted for this chapter is taken from a painting entitled *Mourning for the dead Christ* by the late fifteenth-century Italian artist Pietro Perugino. He hints at the wealth of Joseph by the richness of the fabrics used in his clothing.

Although Joseph of Arimathea's presence in the Gospels is limited to his actions in securing a burial for Jesus, tradition has provided a far more extensive set of connections with Jesus. The very fact that it is Joseph who seeks permission to take the body of Jesus suggests that he may have been a close male relative, in line with the responsibilities of Jewish tradition. This may have given rise to the tradition that Joseph was the uncle of Mary, and great-uncle of Jesus.

His wealth was understood to arise from trade, and significantly in the legends, from trade with the Isles of Britain. At first, this may seem unlikely, but in fact, Britain was one of the few sources of tin available to the Roman world, and tin is essential to the making of bronze. Mining is well attested in Britain from a very early age. The copper mines on the Great Orme in north Wales can be dated back four thousand years, and tin is an abundant metal in Cornwall and an early centre of trade across the entire ancient world.

It is not impossible that Joseph was a wealthy merchant and relative of Jesus with links to Britain. This makes certain legends all the more intriguing. We're told that Joseph brought his young great-nephew on more than one of his trading journeys, and this leads to the legend that Jesus himself visited Britain and blessed it. It is most famously celebrated in the hymn by the early nineteenth-century writer and mystic William Blake, 'Jerusalem'.

After the death of Jesus, Joseph is said to have returned to evangelise Britain, founding the first British Church at Glastonbury. He is reported to have carried with him certain artifacts – a vial of the blood and another of the sweat of Jesus, which were preserved at Glastonbury Abbey in the 1350s; a staff that he planted at Wearyall Hill in Glastonbury, which blossomed into the famous hawthorn tree, a descendent of which blossoms still at Christmas and Easter, and perhaps most significantly, the cup that Jesus used at the Last Supper, the Holy Grail.

IV

Whatever we make of such legends, we can perhaps take away the learning that the early Church may have been quite a tight knit circle of a couple of families, committed to Jesus as much by ties of family as by commitment to Jesus as Messiah. There is the family link with John the Baptist. We know that there were at least two pairs of brothers among the disciples, and possibly one father and son (Jude – not Iscariot – is named as the son of James the Less in some early texts of the Gospels). We've also seen the significance of Mary, the mother of the Lord, for the early Christian community, and the New Testament and early Church histories witness to the fact that James, the brother of Jesus, led the early Church in Jerusalem, being hailed as its first bishop in later generations.

The earliest believers in Jesus lived in community, and community involvement remains important for Christian faith and discipleship to this day. The very name Church goes back to roots that mean 'gathering', and an essential element of being a disciple is to join in with worship in a community that reaches out to others. In becoming Christians, we become part of a community that stretches back through the ages to those first families who put their trust in Jesus.

Dear Lord, help us to be rooted in a Christian community where we can love and be loved, and part of your family. May we nourish and care for others, as Joseph of Arimathea cared for Jesus and the first disciples, and may we find in the Christian community, joy, fellowship and adventure. Amen.

NINETEEN
THE EMPTY TOMB

Holy Saturday, sometimes colloquially but quite incorrectly known as Easter Saturday, is a day of waiting. Jesus had prophesied that in three days he would be raised up (John 2.19), and by the inclusive reckoning used in the ancient world, Sunday is the third day.

I

Modern scholars have largely agreed that Mark is the earliest of the Gospels, based on the rather unrefined Greek and the immediate style of story-telling, and because virtually all the verses of Mark appear almost exactly reproduced in the Gospels according to Matthew and Luke. It is clear that the end of the Gospel was received with dissatisfaction, because the early manuscripts have no fewer than three different endings. Two longer endings add descriptions of appearances of the risen Christ, but the shortest, and possibly original ending, closes abruptly.

Early on the Sunday morning, shortly after sunrise, three of the women disciples bring the spices to anoint Jesus. They haven't given thought about how to enter the sealed tomb, but on arrival, the stone covering the entrance has been rolled away. A young man tells them that Jesus is risen, and that he is not there, but 'going before you into Galilee'. The Gospel ends on a note of astonishment and fear, without resolution. In Luke, two men in dazzling apparel provide scriptural back up for the message, and Peter arrives to inspect the empty tomb. In Matthew, supernatural details are added – an angel, whose appearance is like lightning, descends and rolls away the stone as the women approach.

John gives the longest account, and here there are no angels or men in shining vesture. For John, Mary Magdalene finds the empty tomb, and rushes to find Peter and the disciple whom Jesus loved, who both run to the tomb to discover discarded grave clothes.

The details vary, but all are confident in one proclamation – the tomb is found empty.

II

In the aftermath of the rebellion by the Jewish people against Roman rule in 135 AD, the emperor Hadrian ordered the complete destruction of the ancient city of Jerusalem, and its replacement by a Roman colony named Aelia Capitolina. Hadrian seems to have paid particular attention to the locations that he chose for new temples dedicated to Graeco-Roman deities. The Temple complex was singled out for a sanctuary to Jupiter Capitolinus, the patron God of Rome. To its west, he chose a particular site for a Temple to Aphrodite, his family patron deity, and the patron of Legion X, which was to occupy the city. The early Church historian Eusebius suggests that he did this precisely to fill in a site that included an empty tomb that was already the focus of religious sentiment and pilgrimage. It does make sense that Hadrian was targeting the focus of Christian devotion, which had remembered the empty burial site of Jesus.

Helena, the mother of Constantine, who had discovered Calvary and the relics of the True Cross in the vicinity, now uncovered the empty tomb by demolishing Hadrian's Temple. Once the tomb was located, Helena began its transformation. The limestone escarpment that contained the tomb was cut away to produce a small self-contained shrine, known as the Aedicule, literally 'the little building'. The picture that I have chosen for this chapter is a copy of a mosaic in the Basilica of Sant'Apollinare Nuovo in Ravenna from the sixth century, which depicts the Aedicule as it was remembered by the artist. The ground around was cleared, and a large colonnade and dome built over it. The site has evolved into the Church of the Holy Sepulchre (also known as the Church of the Resurrection).

Down through the centuries, the Aedicule has been ornamented and remodelled, but in 2016, a complete restoration allowed the archaeologists to examine the chamber within it which was reputed to be the tomb of Christ. Beneath the present-day marble cladding, they found a Crusader marble flagstone, and beneath that, a limestone burial shelf dating back to the time of Jesus. History seems to confirm what faith had known. This is the tomb of Jesus.

The Church of the Holy Sepulchre has been a church fought over down through the centuries. Helena and Constantine had constructed a large basilica next to the tomb of Christ and its dome, but this became lost in a series of reconstructions by the Crusaders and others. Today, the pilgrim is greeted by a host of Christian denominations competing for the space: this area is curated by the Greek Orthodox, and that by the Roman Catholic Church. Here is a Coptic shrine, while the Ethiopians have occupied a church built on the roof. So closely fought over have the individual elements been contested that in the eighteenth century, when the church fell within the jurisdiction of the Ottoman Empire, the Sultan determined that every inch of the building would be divided permanently among the different denominations as it was on a particular day in 1757. This led to the intriguing development of the immoveable ladder. It had been left on that day beneath a window and has remained there ever since. Originally used by the Armenians, it can only be moved if absolutely everyone agrees.

For Orthodox Christians, the sanctity of the tomb is vouchsafed by a miracle said to take place every Easter Eve according to the Orthodox calendar. The Patriarch of Jerusalem enters the tomb alone and in the dark, and it is said that holy fire miraculously bathes the stone bed of the tomb, from which the Patriarch lights the first Paschal candle, a living reminder of the Resurrection and the empty tomb.

For some this overlay of history and legend is deeply moving, and it speaks of centuries of devotion. For others, the complexity obscures the story of the Resurrection, and there are some who prefer the Garden Tomb in Jerusalem, another first-century tomb that closely matches the biblical description; it lies just north of the city and does not have the patina of centuries of devotion.

However, the existence of an empty tomb in Jerusalem witnesses to the astounding claim at the heart of Christian belief, that on a particular day, in this particular place, God's saving acts intersected with history to underwrite the promise of eternal life. 'If Christ has not been raised,' wrote the apostle Paul, 'your faith is futile' (1 Corinthians 15.17). The Church of the Holy Sepulchre is the testimony of two millennia to this central belief.

Father God, you so loved the world that you gave us your Son to conquer death and open the gate of everlasting life. Help us to understand and to trust your work of salvation. Amen.

TWENTY

THE RISEN CHRIST

Shortly after the discovery of the empty tomb, the Gospels record that the disciples began to have encounters with Jesus once again – from beyond the death so publicly and uncompromisingly inflicted on Good Friday. What can we say about the risen Lord?

I

The Scriptures are quite clear. The central proclamation of the early Church was that Jesus had risen from the dead. 'Know for certain that God has made him both Lord and Christ, this Jesus whom you crucified' (Acts 2.36). The Resurrection is at the heart of the preaching of the Book of the Acts of the

Apostles, and the central theme of Paul's letters which make up the bulk of the New Testament.

The Gospels go to extraordinary length to stress the physicality of the risen Christ. The disciples are invited to touch him and the wounds left by the crucifixion (Luke 24.39, John 20.27). They eat several meals with him (Luke 24.30, 24.41ff, John 21.10ff). Paul the apostle records a whole string of appearances that for him constitute evidence of the Resurrection: 'For I delivered to you as of first importance what I also received: that Christ died for our sins in accordance with the Scriptures, that he was buried, that he was raised on the third day in accordance with the Scriptures, and that he appeared to Cephas [Peter], then to the twelve. Then he appeared to more than five hundred brothers at one time, most of whom are still alive, though some have fallen asleep. Then he appeared to James, then to all the apostles. Last of all, as to one untimely born, he appeared also to me' (1 Cor. 15.3–8).

The message that the writers of the New Testament wish to convey is that this is no spirit or ghost, but a living, breathing presence, and a sign of the Resurrection promised at the end of time.

At the same time, this is no ordinary body. Jesus can appear behind locked doors (John 20.19) and disappear again. The disciples do not always recognise the person they are encountering, and his appearance seems to have changed (Luke 24.14, 15; John 20.40). Certainly the Jesus encountered in a vision by John, the writer of the Apocalypse, in that book radiates a supernatural authority and presence (Rev. 1.12–16).

By its supernatural nature, the Resurrection of Jesus transcends history, and cannot be proved to a historian's level of satisfaction, although many attempts, such as Frank Morison's *Who moved the Stone?*, have been made.

Perhaps the greatest evidence in its favour is the impact it had on the disciples. Something turned this small, dispirited group of followers into a force that spread the Christian message across the entire Mediterranean within a generation. Charles W Colson, the disgraced American politician and later Christian apologist, is recorded as saying that he believed the Resurrection because he compared the witness of the disciples with those of the twelve politicians caught up in the Watergate scandal. If they had not been able to suppress the truth for even three weeks, he argued, how could the apostles have endured decades of hardship, rejection and persecution and maintained an unbroken witness for the rest of their lives?

Certainly, the evidence of the books of the New Testament, all of which were completed within a hundred years of the Crucifixion, is of a transformed and growing crowd of witnesses who believed that they were experiencing the power and guidance of the Risen Lord in their present lives. Modern scholars have sometimes struggled to explain how the teachings of a thoroughly Jewish rabbi figure, Jesus of Nazareth, gave birth to a religion based on a sacrificial death and a mystical union with a saviour who was hailed as Lord and Christ and understood as God Incarnate. It was surely the early and profound experience and conviction of the Resurrection of Jesus that turned the focus from the teaching of Jesus to the significance of the person of Jesus himself.

The picture of the Risen Lord with which I have opened this chapter is adapted from a fourteenth-century fresco of the Anastasis (the Orthodox term for the Resurrection) in the Church of the Holy Saviour in present day Istanbul. Depictions of the Anastasis vary from Western images of the Resurrection in that they depict a supernatural element in the story of the Resurrection – the Harrowing of Hell. This tradition arises from obscure verses among the letters of the New Testament. 1 Peter includes this phrase: 'Christ ... being put to death in the flesh but made alive in the spirit ... went and preached to the spirits in prison' (1 Peter 3.18, 19). In the letter to the Ephesians, the apostle Paul, quoting scripture, writes, 'When he ascended on high he led a host of captives, and he gave gifts to men. In saying "He ascended", what does it mean but that he had also descended into the lower regions of the earth?' (Ephesians 4.8, 9).

Reflecting on these Scriptures, and asking what happened to the Saviour between death and resurrection, the tradition evolved that Jesus went to the lowest regions of the realm of the dead and released all who were held captive there. In icons of the Anastasis Jesus bursts from the tomb, and Satan and the doors of Hell are shown broken beneath his feet. In his hands, he grasps Adam and Eve, raising them from imprisonment and freeing them into the reality of entry into heaven.

IV

'Thanks be to God, who in Christ always leads us in triumphal procession' (2 Corinthians 2.14). For the Christian, the Resurrection is the sign of our redemption and the firm foundation of our hope. As Christ was liberated from death, and death could not hold him, so there is the promise, not just of eternal life, but of freedom from the chains of sin and oppression that can so tightly ensnare us. The Christian is always free to begin again by God's grace and power.

This is the Easter proclamation, which calls us to renew our own commitment of faith. The risen Lord himself says to us: 'Fear not, I am the first and the last, and the living one. I died, and behold I am alive for evermore, and I have the keys of Death and Hades' (Revelation 1.17, 18).

Lord Jesus, teach us to believe and trust in your resurrection from the dead. Enable us to be freed from all that holds us back, and to follow you until we come at last to that place which you prepare for us. Amen.

TWENTY-ONE
MARY MAGDALEN

We have noticed how women play a significant role in Jesus' ministry – some anonymous and some named. One of the most significant, however, and recorded as the first witness to encounter the risen Lord, is Mary Magdalen.

I

Many stories are told about Mary Magdalen, and she is named twelve times across the four Gospels. She appears to have been rescued by Jesus from a miserable existence, and both Mark and Luke record that Jesus had driven seven possessing demons out of her (Luke 8.2, Mark 16.9). This meant that for many years, the Church, led by the thinking of Pope St Gregory the Great, identified her with the woman who anointed Jesus' feet with perfume, and the woman caught in adultery. Although Matthew, Mark and John place the anointing late in Jesus' ministry, as discussed earlier, Luke tells the story earlier in his Gospel, and offers an insight into the woman as a 'sinful woman', whose reputation causes Simon the Pharisee to question Jesus' discernment.

She clearly travelled with Jesus (Luke 8.1–3), and appears alongside Jesus throughout the story of the Passion, being one of those standing near the cross during Jesus' execution (Matthew 27.56, Mark 15.40 and John 19.25).

In John's Gospel, it is Mary who first comes to the tomb on Easter morning, and who discovers it empty (John 20.1). In Matthew's account, she is accompanied by another Mary, who is then named by Mark as Mary, the mother of James, and who adds a third woman, Salome, whom Luke identifies as Joanna. They believe the news of the Resurrection, in stark contrast to the disciples, who are depicted as fearful and unready to believe.

II

The fullest story is told by John, where Mary, having reported the empty tomb to the disciples Peter and John, stands in the garden weeping (John 20.11–18). There she encounters the risen Lord, but, in her sorrow, confuses him with the gardener. It is only when Jesus calls her by name that she realises who he is. Although John does not mention it, the other evangelists speak of her clinging to Jesus' feet, and Jesus has to ask her in John's account not to hold on to him (John 20.17). Commentators have seen this not as a rebuff, but rather an allusion to the fact that Jesus will not physically remain among his disciples. This scene has become a favourite for Christian art, and is known as 'Noli me Tangere', the

Latin for 'Do not hold onto me.' The portrait I offer of Mary is adapted from the famous rendition of this scene by the fourteenth-century artist Giotto in the Magdalen Chapel of the Basilica of St Francis at Assisi.

Mary's name is understood as giving her town of origin, Magdala, which was an anciently founded city on the shore of the Sea of Galilee, and the centre of some remarkable recent excavations that have revealed the town that Mary knew.

III

We have noted that Mary Magdalen was understood as the woman caught in adultery, and therefore in Christian tradition she gained a reputation as a reformed prostitute, although the identification is probably insecure. The high significance placed on her presence among Jesus' disciples in the four Gospels, however, led to speculation as to her real significance. The apocryphal Gospel of Philip mentions that she was often close to Jesus, and that Jesus even kissed her on several occasions.

At this point, some modern writers have put two and two together, and made five. Since it was highly unusual for people to remain unmarried in the first century in the Holy Land, people have speculated that Jesus ought to have married, and that Mary Magdalen is the chief suspect for his wife. This is taken to great lengths in pseudo-histories like *The Holy Blood and the Holy Grail* and even fiction like Dan Brown's *Da Vinci Code*, to suggest that the children of this union formed a sacred bloodline that survived down to later generations.

Two, more ancient, traditions survive – one that Mary Magdalen went to Ephesus after the Resurrection, with the Mother of Jesus and the disciple John, and there is even some suggestion that she was betrothed to John. The other has her joining Lazarus' journey to southern France, with La-Sainte-Baume, near Marseilles, being named as the location of her death, burial and relics.

IV

These intense speculations perhaps sensationalise a saint, whose primary witness is to the Resurrection. It is interesting that the first witnesses of the Resurrection are all women, at a time when women's testimony was not as trusted as that of male witnesses. Some have seen Mary Magdalen as the first apostle, sent by Jesus to proclaim the Resurrection to the disciples. At the very least, this recognition should challenge the attitudes of the Church towards women. The Church has been too ready to downgrade women to ancillary positions and ministries. There is great irony in this, when women are often in the majority of many congregations, and chief among those bearing witness to the gospel through their own ministry and activities.

As we draw this reflection to a close, let us give thanks for all the great women whose witness to faith has helped us in our journey of discipleship.

Lord Jesus, as you called Mary Magdalen to be the first witness to the Resurrection, free us from the discrimination and bias shown against women down through the centuries. Help the Church to be a community of women and men, where the work of the Holy Spirit may be recognised equally in our lives. Amen.

TWENTY-TWO
JOHN THE BELOVED DISCIPLE

Another of the disciples closely associated with the events of
Easter Day is John. Gauging his importance to the biblical
story, however, depends on one crucial identification. John, the
son of Zebedee, is clearly listed among the Twelve, who are the
closest disciples of Jesus. His name, however, is less apparent
in John's Gospel, in which there are many references to 'the
disciple whom Jesus loved' instead. If the presumed author of
the Gospel and the disciple enrolled among the Twelve are the
same person, however, this may have been a way of the author
of the Gospel being coy about his testimony.

If we accept this identification, then in the Gospels, John is another disciple who plays a very significant role. He is among the first to follow Jesus (John 1.35), on the recommendation of John the Baptist. He formed one of the closest circles of disciples of Jesus, being part of the group known as the Three (Peter, James and John). They alone witness the raising of Jairus' daughter (Mark 5.37), the Transfiguration of Jesus on the Mount (Matthew 17.1) and the agonising prayer of Jesus in the Garden of Gethsemane the night of his betrayal (Matthew 26.37).

John plays a significant role in the events of the last week of Jesus' life, being sent with Peter to prepare the Last Supper (Luke 22.8), and reclines closest to him at the supper itself (John 13.23). It is John who secures entry for himself and Peter to the High Priest's house at the time of the trial (John 18.15, 16). As we have seen, he stands with the Mother of Jesus at the foot of the cross, and Jesus commends his mother into his care (John 19.26, 27).

In John's Gospel chapter 20, Mary Magdalen reports to John and Peter when she finds the empty tomb, before her own encounter with Jesus. Peter is the first to enter the tomb, but again it is the beloved disciple who first understands what is going on, and believes (John 20.8).

II & III

John's Gospel often gives a different version of events from the three Gospels of Matthew, Mark and Luke, which can be read side by side. Because the quality of the Greek is so much more polished, and the Gospel filled with theological reflection, it is generally dated as the last of the canonical Gospels, around 100 AD.

Its internal witness, however, sounds much earlier. It has details that sound like personal testimony, and follows the convention of talking about the experiences that might be witnessed by the author in the third person, 'the beloved disciple'. Three times, in John's Gospel, the writer addresses his readers directly – John 19.35, where he offers testimony to the spear thrust at the crucifixion, and in John 20.30, 31, where he speaks of the purpose of the Gospel. In the last chapter of John (chapter 21), the writer speaks a third time to his readership to clarify a saying of Jesus, arguing that it was not a prophecy about John's immortality (John 21.22, 23). Verse 24 is particularly interesting, because it appears to include a comment by some of the earliest readers: 'This is the disciple who is bearing witness about these things, and we know that his testimony is true.'

At least one significant scholar (John Robinson) sees such details as betraying an early origin for John, with significant elements of authenticity. Certainly, it would tie in with the tradition that John retired to Ephesus, and lived there a long time into old age. Irenaeus, one of the earliest Church teachers whose writings have survived, and who lived in the second century, recounts a story he had heard from Polycarp, who had witnessed it for himself, about John at Ephesus, and in Jerome John is recorded as an old blind man, repeating what he had heard from Jesus to anyone who would listen, 'Little children, love one another.'

John was reputedly the youngest of Jesus' disciples, and in Christian art, is often shown as a clean-shaven young man, as opposed to the older and bearded disciples among whom he finds his place. I have based my picture of John on his appearance in the painting SS *John and Peter at the Tomb of Christ* by the seventeenth-century Italian artist Giovanni Francesco Romanelli.

IV

The book of the Apocalypse speaks, in a vision of the throne of God, about the throne being supported by four angelic animals: a man, a lion, an ox and an eagle (Revelation 4.6–8). Over time, and with the acceptance of the four Gospels as authoritative, each of the animals became linked with one of the Gospels. The eagle was assigned to John's Gospel. This was, later Christian symbolists argued, because the eagle as a bird flew highest into heaven and had the sharpest sight, and John, as an evangelist, plumbed deeper into the mysteries of Christ, and portrayed the most compelling of Jesus' portraits.

The example of John stands for us as one who sought to understand Jesus, and invited us to believe: 'These [signs] are written so that you may believe that Jesus is the Christ, the Son of God, and that by believing you may have life in his name' (John 20.31).

Let us pray that like John, we may desire to see Jesus clearly, and to understand his teachings. Let us pray that we may take to heart the lesson that he taught, that we might love one another, and that like John, we may know ourselves to be beloved by God.

Lord God, you gave to John the gift of faith in the risen Lord, and through him, have taught us that in Jesus is the way of true life. Inspire us to follow in his footsteps, to know Jesus in our lives, and to reflect his love in the world. Amen.

TWENTY-THREE
PETER THE APOSTLE

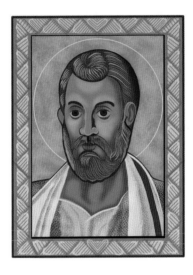

Another member of the Three is Simon, to whom Jesus gave a new name, Peter, the Rock. What part does Peter play in the story of the Passion and Resurrection?

I

Among the first of the disciples called according to all four Gospels, and playing a significant role, is Simon Peter. Peter comes across in the Gospels as ebullient, frank and given to the big gesture, a characteristic that sometimes gets him in trouble. At the Last Supper, for example, Peter protests that he will not let his Lord wash his feet (John 13.1–17). When Jesus insists on the value of his action, Peter goes to the other extreme, suggesting that he should submit his hands and head for washing also.

Perhaps the clearest and most famous way in which the theme of transformation is recorded, however, is in the difference between Peter before and after the Passion and Resurrection. At the Last Supper, Jesus predicts that he will be betrayed, provoking yet another outburst from Peter that he will never abandon Jesus. Sharply, Jesus predicts that Peter will deny him before twenty-four hours are out (Matthew 26.31–35, Mark 14.27–31, Luke 22.31–38, John 13.37, 38). So it comes to pass. Simon Peter is bold enough to follow Jesus into the house of the High Priests, but when challenged, disassociates himself from his teacher (Matthew 26.69–75, Mark 14.66–72, Luke 22.55–62 and John 18.15–18).

Many students of Scripture have noticed, however, the gentle way with which the risen Jesus deals with Peter in John 21.15–19. Peter is asked three times whether he loves Jesus, and is given the chance to affirm his love. It is a much chastened and more cautious Peter who replies, but who is confirmed by Jesus in his role as pastor to the Church.

Although this story is well known, I cannot ever read it without taking note of the gentleness and love of our Lord. He does not call us to be faultless in our discipleship, but takes care to restore us and transform us by his love.

II

Peter has left his footprint more indelibly in the archaeological record than any other disciple. The Gospels record that Jesus was living in Capernaum at the start of his ministry, and it was here that Jesus recruited Simon Peter as a disciple.

In the twentieth century, a team of Italian archaeologists made a series of spectacular discoveries in their excavations of the town. They first uncovered the remains of an octagonal church dating to the fifth century, dedicated to Peter. On further investigation, beneath it, they found the remains of a first-century home, a rather mundane relic from Jesus' time. What was transformative, however, was the way in which the house had been restored at the end of the first century. The main room of the house had been freshly plastered, a rare occurrence for simple homes. Large storage jars and lamps had been moved into the building, and ultimately there was evidence that the main room had been used for gathering of Christian worship. More than a hundred graffiti had been scratched into the walls, saying 'Christ have mercy' or similar exhortations in Greek, Syriac and Hebrew. The archaeologists even discerned references to the apostle Peter. Could this then, have been the original home of the apostle?

In Rome as well, archaeologists in the twentieth century have investigated the site believed to be the Tomb of Peter beneath St Peter's Basilica. Many layers of devotion were uncovered, but at the earliest level, human remains were found, which Pope Paul VI concluded might reliably be the bones of Peter. A set of bones found in a niche on the north side of the archaeological remains were identified as the bones of a man aged between sixty and seventy from the first century AD.

Of course, it is almost impossible to find absolute proof for either of these finds. It is not unreasonable to conclude, however, that perhaps the original home of the fisherman from Galilee has been found as well as his final resting place. I find it incredibly moving that between these remains the story of Peter is sketched out, of the fisherman of Galilee who ended his days as a faithful 'fisher of men' and witness to the Resurrection.

III

The tradition that Peter died in Rome is an ancient one. Jesus himself prophesied that Peter would suffer in his old age, and that his hands would be stretched out (John 21.18,19). Early tradition asserted that Peter had met his death by crucifixion at Rome during the persecution unleased by the emperor Nero after the Great Fire of Rome in 64 AD. The Letter of Clement, dating to the end of the first century, speaks of Peter as having been martyred in Rome, and a similar witness is provided by Tertullian, a writer of the second century. Origen, writing at about the same time, reports that Peter was crucified, but that, because he did not feel that he was worthy of dying in the same manner as his Lord, he asked to be crucified upside down.

In the apocryphal 'Acts of Peter' the story is told that Peter originally intended to flee the persecution, and that he actually started on his journey from Rome. As he departs, he encounters the risen Christ, carrying his cross and walking into the city. In the famous phrase Peter asks, '*Domine, quo vadis?*' – Lord, where are you going? – only to be told that Christ is going into Rome to be crucified again in the persecution of the Church. This convinces Peter that he must return and share the suffering that is being meted out to God's people.

IV

In Peter, we are brought face to face again with the very fragile nature of discipleship. The picture I have adapted for this chapter is taken from a very early icon of Peter, preserved from the sixth century in the Monastery of St Catherine at the foot of Mount Sinai. It shows, I believe, a very human Peter, the gruff fisherman transformed by God's grace to be a leader of the Church. It inspires us in realistic discipleship, where we are not called to be perfect, but by God's power to be transformed into faithful servants. May God's power be at work in us as it was in Peter.

Lord Jesus Christ, you called and empowered Peter to leave his nets and to follow you. In the same way, reveal to us your vocation, and forever strengthen us to be worthy disciples and servants. Amen.

TWENTY-FOUR
EMMAUS

Luke's Gospel tells an extended story about one Resurrection appearance by Jesus, which happened on a walk to the village of Emmaus (Luke 24.13–35). What happened and why is this significant?

I

Luke tells us that two of the disciples were walking to a village about seven miles outside Jerusalem. Only one of them is named Cleopas, whose wife, Mary, had been among the women at the cross. Jesus joins them as they walk, but they do not recognise him, as they discuss the events of the last few days. The disciples are astounded that their companion does not appear to know what has been happening. As they explain their hope that Jesus would have been the Messiah, and their bewilderment at the rumours of the empty tomb, their companion explains to them the Scriptures and interprets how they point to Jesus and the events of the last week. They beg their fellow traveller to join them for supper, but once there, the way in which Jesus breaks bread and offers it to them – presumably reminding them of the events just four days earlier – reveals who it is that is travelling with them.

II

There are a number of locations that have been identified as the ancient Emmaus, with the excavations at Imwas having most historical support, revealing remains of churches from the sixth and twelfth centuries, although there are other locations that fit the details of Luke's account.

The story is another favourite in Christian art, and there are many representations of the event by some of the greatest artists of the sixteenth and seventeenth centuries. Such pictures tend to focus on the moment when Jesus blesses and breaks bread and is recognised by the two disciples.

The picture that I have chosen for this chapter is an adaptation once again from the Bible of the Hague, a thirteenth-century illustrated Bible. In it, the figure of Jesus breaks the bread, while the two disciples, both in distinctive Jewish travelling clothes, suddenly realise who it is with them.

III

Once again, the story emphasises the physicality and strangeness of the risen Christ. He walks and talks with the disciples for some considerable period – this is no mere apparition – and then stays and eats with them. Yet the disciples do not recognise him – the passage says that they were prevented from recognising him – and at the end of the story we are simply told that Jesus disappeared.

Although the story operates as one of the Resurrection appearances, it perhaps hints at something bigger – in future the disciples are to recognise Jesus in Word and Sacrament, rather than in his physical presence.

It is notable how Luke talks about the reaction of the disciples after Jesus has left them: 'Did not our hearts burn within us while he talked to us on the road, while he opened to us the scriptures?' (Luke 24.32). Jesus had 'beginning with Moses and all the Prophets, ... interpreted to them in all the scriptures the things concerning himself' (Luke 24.27), and this would have been reflected in the practice of the early Church, who would have gathered for the reading of the Bible (in its Jewish form at this stage). They would have interpreted the writings in the light of their experience of Jesus, as illustrated in the Book of the Acts. In time, writings that the early Church were confident could be traced back to the apostles and their companions were added to the Scriptures to produce what we now know as the New Testament, but with the same purpose: to remember Jesus, and the way in which the revelation of God in him should be proclaimed.

In the same way, it is significant that the disciples recognised Jesus in the breaking of the bread. Acts chapter 2 records that the four marks of the worship of the early Church were 'the apostles' teaching, the fellowship, the breaking of bread and the prayers' (Acts 2.42), and the breaking of bread is mentioned as significant a number of times in the Book of Acts. This suggests more than merely sharing a meal. The events of the Last Supper have begun to be repeated as a regular feature of Church life and worship, and are seen again as an occasion when Jesus may be recognised in the presence of the Church.

The apostle Paul, writing in his first letter to the early Church in Corinth speaks of passing on to them what he received directly from the Lord – the tradition of repeating the elements of the Last Supper and the blessing and consumption of bread and wine (1 Corinthians 11.20–26). He has already described this meal as a recognition of Christ's presence: 'The cup of blessing that we bless, is it not a participation in the blood of Christ? The bread that we break, is it not a participation in the body of Christ?' (1 Corinthians 10.16). Several theologians have noted that this formula reads almost like a quotation from a liturgy of the early Church, but whatever we believe, it is evidence that the Church from the beginning recognised Jesus in the breaking of bread.

IV

In the same way that the earliest disciples were recognisable by what they did, so the Church down through the centuries has followed similar patterns. They have gathered to read the Scriptures and to celebrate the sacraments, and it is one of the ways in which the Church may be recognised. Anglicans even enshrined this in their official teaching in the sixteenth century: 'The visible Church of God is a congregation of faithful men [Yes, I'm afraid that the language of the articles is very sixteenth century in its prejudices] in which the pure Word of God is preached, and the Sacraments be duly ministered according to Christ's ordinance' (Article XIX of the Thirty-Nine Articles).

However, this was nothing new. Pliny the Younger, Roman Governor and author, recorded in the second century that it was the custom of Christians to gather before dawn, to sing hymns 'to Christ as to a God', to commit themselves to turning away from sin, and to partake of food as their regular practice.

'Let us consider how to stir up one another to love and good works', wrote the author of the Letter to the Hebrews in the New Testament, 'not neglecting to meet together' (Hebrews 10.24, 25). We now are invited to enter into this tradition, to join ourselves to the family of the living Christ, which has extended across the world and down through the centuries, and to experience for ourselves the power of the Resurrection in our lives. Let us pray that we may not neglect this channel of divine grace and love, by which God may refresh us.

Lord God, as your Son revealed himself to the disciples at Emmaus through the breaking of the bread, so come to us as we gather as your family in the Church. Make yourself known to us in Word and Sacrament, that we may know your risen power. Amen.

TWENTY-FIVE
THE ROBIN

In his Letter to the Church at Rome, Paul wrote about the universal significance of the saving work of God:

> 'For the creation waits with eager longing for the revealing of the sons of God. For the creation was subjected to futility, not willingly, but because of him who subjected it in the hope that the creation itself will be set free from its bondage to corruption and obtain the freedom of the glory of the children of God.' (Romans 8.19–21)

I think it was the Christian thinker and Oxford academic CS Lewis who wrote that if God revealed himself in death and Resurrection, then we should expect that pattern to be repeated throughout creation. Lewis saw the pattern of the seasons, of the annual dying of autumn and resurrection of spring to be evidence of this pattern, and the echoes of God's revelation in Christ in many other religions and traditions.

In the same way, the medieval mind was fertile in observing nature and finding links with the divine. We have already noticed how the dorsal marking of the donkey was interpreted as the sign of the cross, left as tribute to the master who once rode on a donkey, and many elements of creation were thought to reflect the story of the Passion.

One such story is the story of the robin. Noticing its red breast, some Christian somewhere made a link with the story of the cross and gave birth to a legend. The robin has a red breast, it was narrated, because, while Jesus was crucified, a robin had perched upon the cross and plucked a thorn from the crown adorning Jesus' brow. As it flew away, the thorn had caught Jesus, and a few drops of blood had coloured the breast of the robin, which was now forever red with the blood of the Saviour.

This quaint but curious legend reminds us that the eye of faith may find evidence of the Passion and Resurrection of Jesus everywhere. More seriously, it is a reminder that God wants us to discover new life in all of creation, and for us to be released into the glorious liberty of the Children of God, which is the destiny that God intends for us all. All creation sings the glory of Easter.

As Richard Hoyle translated the words of the French hymn by Edmond Budry:

Lo, Jesus meets us, risen from the tomb,
Lovingly he greets us, scatters fear and gloom.
Let the Church with gladness hymns of triumph sing,
For Her Lord now liveth; death hath lost its sting.

ABOUT PARACLETE PRESS

PARACLETE PRESS is the publishing arm of the Cape Cod Benedictine community, the Community of Jesus. Presenting a full expression of Christian belief and practice, we reflect the ecumenical charism of the Community and its dedication to sacred music, the fine arts, and the written word.

Learn more about us at our website:

SCAN
TO
READ

www.paracletepress.com

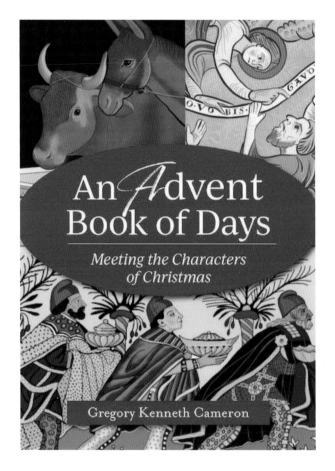